COMMUNICATION FOR PROBLEM SOLVING

COMMUNICATION FOR PROBLEM SOLVING

DAN B. CURTIS, Ph. D.
Head of the Department of Speech Communication
Central Missouri State University—Warrensburg

JOSEPH M. MAZZA, Ph. D.
Assistant Professor of Speech Communication
Central Missouri State University—Warrensburg

STEPHEN RUNNEBOHM, Ph. D.
Associate Professor of Speech Communication
University of Arkansas—Little Rock

John Wiley & Sons, Inc., Publishers
New York • Chichester • Brisbane • Toronto

Publisher: Judy Wilson
Editor: Irene Brownstone
Production Manager: Ken Burke
Copy Editor: Gail Larrick
Makeup: Wendy Welsh

Library of Congress Cataloging in Publication Data:

Curtis, Dan B
    Communication for problem solving.

    (Wiley self-teaching guides)
    Includes index.
    1. Problem solving, Group. 2. Discussion.
I. Mazza, Joseph M., joint author. II. Runnebohm,
Stephen, joint author. III. Title.
HM133.C87   301.18'5   79-18487
ISBN 0-471-02132-6

Printed in the United States of America

79 80   10   9   8   7   6   5   4   3   2   1

Acknowledgments

We are grateful to many people for their assistance and support of our efforts in writing this book. We want to thank the administrative staff at Central Missouri State University (CMSU) and the University of Arkansas at Little Rock for their encouragement and support. We wish to thank graduate students and faculty at CMSU who have helped by critiquing portions of our work. We are particularly grateful to Dr. James Floyd of the Speech Communication faculty at CMSU and to Dr. Joe McAdoo, Chairman of the Communication Department of Drury College for use of original case studies and to Mike Davis, Derald Harris, Alec McCommon, and Bill Wallace, all graduate students at CMSU, for their contributions to the book.

A special appreciation goes to Dr. James Bibson, Chairman of the Speech and Dramatic Arts Department at the University of Missouri, Columbia, for providing the stimulus to begin the project; and a special note of thanks to Dr. Richard Thiede for his contributions which gave impetus to the developmental stage of the text.

Finally to our colleagues in our respective departments and to Linda Curtis and Idy Mazza, we say thanks for the persistent encouragement for us to complete the writing, even though it meant that other equally important projects at the office and in the home were temporarily relegated to the proverbial "back burner."

Preface

"Talk, talk, talk! That seems to be all we ever accomplish; we never do anything constructive about solving our problems." Such an observation is frequently made and and too often true, but seldom do we seek ways to alleviate the "talk, talk, talk" frustration.

As our society grows larger and its structure more complex, the need for effective group cooperation becomes essential. Many of us have been involved in situations where such cooperation was needed to solve complex problems—and the lack of it resulted in catastrophe. If only the college officials and students at Kent State and Jackson State had operated effectively as problem-solving groups, perhaps the loss of life and the destruction of property could have been avoided.

In our daily routines, we are all involved to some extent in group projects. Effective small group discussion is the key to successful problem solving and decision making in colleges and universities, government, business and industry, church organizations, and literally every existing club and organization. The question is this: How many truly functional groups have you participated in? If your answer is "few, if any," Communication for Problem Solving is for you. This book is designed to give you the concepts and skills you need to organize successful groups and to be an effective group participant. It will not solve all the communications problems in our complex society, but it will offer you ways to structure and organize group encounters in order to make them as practical and functional as possible.

Communication for Problem Solving is designed so that you apply the material as you learn it. Each chapter presents concepts and skills dealing with various aspects of the small group discussion process. The material is presented in numbered segments called frames, including case studies, examples, and questions that allow you to apply the material. For the most effective learning, you should answer the questions before you look at the authors' answer given below the line of dashes. If your response disagrees with the answer provided, review earlier frames until you fully understand the material before you go on.

Because each section builds on earlier sections, you should read the book in sequence, rather than skipping around. However, the index in the back of the book will help you locate specific topics for later reference. In each chapter you will find a list of specific objectives at the beginning, and a self-test at the end, to help you evaluate your progress. At the end of the book is a Final Self-Test for an overall evaluation.

The case studies and examples presented throughout the book should help you apply what you learn about group communication to problem solving and decision making in real-life situations. We hope that you enjoy and profit from your journey through Communication for Problem Solving.

Dan Curtis

Joe Mazza

Steve Runnebohm

Contents

CHAPTER ONE

The Nature of
Problem-Solving Discussion

Few individuals live out their lives without being part of one or more groups.
Perhaps one of the most telling signs of the human need for group membership
is the dread of exclusion from or ostracism by groups. Achieving membership
in the "right" high school club, campus fraternity, or business association can
sometimes become an obsession. If you were to compile a list of all the groups
to which you belong, either actively or casually, the length of that list would
probably surprise you. In a lifetime, an average person associates with family groups, social and fraternal groups, service groups, therapy and training
groups, religious groups, work groups, and task groups, among others. Obviously, not all groups are problem-solving or decision-making groups. Many
groups exist to satisfy the social and emotional needs of their membership;
other activities are labeled as "discussion" when very little discussion takes
place.

Chapter 1 will focus on the characteristics of problem-solving discussion
groups. People often take potshots at problem-solving discussion, saying it's
slow, cumbersome, and frustrating. "I'd rather do the job myself than wait
for a committee to discuss the problem and take action" is a typical comment.
Are such indictments against group problem solving warranted? All too often
they are. But we will explore how a group of people can intelligently examine a
a problem, develop insightful, workable solutions, and implement them in a
commendable, efficient manner.

OBJECTIVES

When you have completed this chapter, you will be able to:

- Identify and describe the essential components of a discussion.

- Distinguish between problem-solving group discussion and other
  activities labeled as discussion.

• Recognize when problem-solving group discussion aids individual problem solving by making better use of human resources.

• Distinguish between public and private discussions.

• Identify the factors that contribute to becoming a group.

WHAT IS PROBLEM-SOLVING DISCUSSION?

1. We all talk with others about ideas that interest us. When that talk channels into a purposeful direction and we probe deeply in an inquisitive, cooperative fashion, our sharing of ideas becomes what we call discussion. Discussion may be defined as a communication process involving a group of people, usually under the direction of a leader, who are working together toward a solution to a problem. In short, discussion is a serious sharing of information designed to help solve a specific problem.

When we say discussion is a communication process, we mean that the participants interact with one another in an effort to establish common meanings and understandings through verbal and nonverbal stimuli. For effective interaction to take place, communication must involve both speaking and listening. All of us have grunted and nodded, making little effort to recognize one another beyond amenities such as "Hi" or "How ya doin'" or "Nice weather, isn't it." (Note that we don't even voice a question mark after the two questions, because we generally don't expect a real response.) In these cases no reciprocal influence results; that is, person A does not influence person B, nor is person B influenced by person A. For meaningful communication to take place in a group, the interaction must involve each person in influencing and being influenced by each other person.

Examine the following situations. In which situation is real group interaction occurring?

_____ (a) Joe sees Mary, with whom he wishes to speak; so he approaches her. Mary, seemingly unaware of Joe's existence, passes him by without the slightest recognition.

__b__ (b) Joe sees Mary, with whom he wishes to speak. Mary notices Joe approaching her and advances expectantly in his direction. Joe smiles as he realizes they soon will be together.

- - - - - - - - - - - - - - - - - -

(b) Mutual influence is experienced by both Joe and Mary in their effort to engage one another, while in (a) Mary was not influenced by Joe.

2. Let's look at another situation which illuminates the concept of interaction. Remember, the essential ingredient is mutual influence. Which of the following situations reveals a greater sense of group interaction?

_____ (a) Susan is a mischievous child in the fifth-grade reading class. She looks out the window, nonverbally implying that something of great interest is passing. Subsequently, both Linda and James begin looking out the window with great anticipation.

✓ (b) Tom, wise to Susan's antics, decides to try the same ploy with two boys he dislikes. Instead, his two closest friends walk over to the window, oblivious to the teacher's reprimand of their actions. Tom realizes with dismay what he has done and apologizes to each of the two boys as they all three walk to the principal's office.

- - - - - - - - - - - - - - - - - - -

(b) Tom was influenced to interact with his friends about a common problem, while in (a) Susan was not influenced by the other two children.

3. Which of the following interactions is what we call a discussion?

✓ (a) During the evening meal Linda asks, "Grant, how did school go today?" Grant replies, "Fine, Mom—except the principal says I am to stay home for three weeks because I was exposed to swine flu today." Dad chimes in. "You were? Tell us what happened." Grant replies, "Well, Dad, we were playing outside when..."

_____ (b) TRA customer-relations person (answering the phone): "TRA passenger refunds and records, Tom Rile speaking. May I help you?" Customer: "I'm sorry, Mr. Rile, I was calling for TBA Cab Service. Please forgive me for dialing the wrong number."

- - - - - - - - - - - - - - - - - - -

(a) The family's interaction during the meal would be considered a discussion, because it is serious, purposeful, and reciprocal.

FEEDBACK

4. One very important extension of interaction in a discussion is feedback. Feedback in a discussion may be defined as a cycle involving an initial stimulus statement from one person, followed by a response from a second person, leading to a response from the first. Feedback, then, is a circular process from A to B to A and so on. The term feedback statement refers to the individual responses in the cycle. Essentially, feedback provides a regulatory influence on interaction. The responses of acceptance or rejection (smiles, nods, statements, frowns, and so on) indicate what modifications people need to make in subsequent interactions.

Many different kinds of feedback statements can be used in a group discussion. Feedback can be very personal: "I wish I had your ability to think through a problem." Feedback can ask for clarification: "Could you please explain your last point?" Questioning is another kind of feedback: "Have you considered the consequences of your proposal?" Another role of feedback is expansion of the initial idea: "If we increase the scope of your plan to involve the whole company, our problem might be solved."

Feedback statements can be divided into two categories—positive and negative. Positive feedback statements contain such elements as encouragement, relevance, thoughtfulness, and brevity. Negative feedback statements include such elements as personal attacks, irrelevance, lack of structure, and excessive length. Positive feedback, by its nature, tends to facilitate the group discussion process. Personal encouragement keeps group members' involvement at a high level—a person who feels he or she is contributing important information and ideas to the group will continue to contribute. Relevant feedback focuses the discussion on the problem at hand and thus provides greater task efficiency. When the feedback statement is brief and thoughtful, the participants in the discussion will be best able to understand and react to the response, thus facilitating the problem-solving process.

Negative feedback statements usually hinder the group discussion process. Personal attacks tend to produce a defensive feeling in the group members. This feeling causes participants either to retreat into silence or to strike back at other members. This type of reaction lowers group efficiency. When the feedback response bears no relation to the initial statement, the participants are likely to become confused. A lengthy, rambling, fragmented response also confuses, irritates, and bores the other members of the group.

The following case illustrates these basic principles of group feedback. Read the case, and then apply the information to the questions at the end.

Case

The Community Betterment Association of a small midwestern town met to discuss the problem of an unsightly parking lot adjoining the town's old railroad depot. Harry, the chairman of the association and a local used car salesman, called the meeting to order. He explained that the parking lot had been used extensively while the railroad operated the depot, but now that the depot was no longer used, the parking lot served only the workers at a small jacket factory who used it for parking, and some local farmers, who used it as a common market for their garden crops. Harry also noted that the parking lot had been taken over by a third group—the teenagers who used it as their nightly gathering place. The purpose of the meeting was to determine if the area could be beautified, and if so, how.

Ruth, a supervisor at the factory, asked how the group members could reach a solution that would satisfy the vastly different groups. When she concluded, Harry noted that Ruth's question should be carefully considered during discussion of the problem.

Mary, a housewife, suggested that the group should first consider the characteristics of the groups using the parking lot before considering possible solutions. John, a retired policeman, stated that the factory workers and farmers were respectable, hard-working citizens who wanted an open place in which to park their cars or sell their goods. The teenagers, he continued, were just a bunch of drunken bums who wanted nothing more than a place to meet, drink, and cause trouble. The problem with this new generation was that they had no respect for their elders and other people's property, he said.

In his day, kids played practical jokes, but no teenager purposely damaged anyone else's land by leaving beer cans, whiskey bottles, and broken glass scattered around. What the town needed, he concluded, was not a pretty parking lot but a mandatory 7:30 p.m. curfew. Mary commented that John's perception of the teenagers' use of the parking lot was not entirely accurate, and that all of them need not be punished because of the manners of a few. The curfew, she continued, would not solve the problem of the deteriorating parking lot or of the abandoned depot.

Roger, a landscape architect, revealed that he had drawn a few sketches of what could be done with the lot. His plans included resurfacing the parking lot with hot-mix asphalt, painting lines to designate parking spaces and market areas, and placing through the lot a center median containing flowers, evergreens, and mercury flood lights. These improvements, he added, would beautify the area, increase its efficiency, and discourage the vandalism John had mentioned. Roger's plan was heartily endorsed by Wayne, a local merchant, as a comprehensive program indicating much thought and work on Roger's part. Wayne did point out, however, that the plans did not include the old depot. He proposed that the association vote to proceed with Roger's suggestions, while also encouraging the railroad company to renovate the old depot as an historical structure. Roger agreed that Wayne's ideas were compatable with his own and that he would be glad to contact the railroad.

Harry then cautioned the group not to get too enthusiastic about the proposal until they had found out how much it would cost and if other solutions might be just as effective and less expensive. Wayne immediately replied that only a fool would assume that a landscape architect would propose something other than the best and most economical solution. He added that if the group did not immediately accept the proposals he and Roger had submitted, he would never buy another car from Harry. The meeting then deteriorated into angry shouts, confusion, and insults.

(a) What feedback role did Ruth's response play?

(b) Was this role positive or negative? _____

(c) Is it true or false that John's comments acted to facilitate the group process? _____

(d) What two characteristics of negative feedback are displayed by John's statements?

(e) Explain how Wayne's response to Roger's proposal aided the group process.

(f) Is it true or false that Harry's response to Wayne's suggestions illustrates clarifying feedback? _____

(g) Explain why the final interaction between Harry and Wayne is not illustrative of the feedback cycle.

(h) Why did the group react so violently to Wayne's last response?

- - - - - - - - - - - - - - - - - -

(a) questioning
(b) Positive. It served to facilitate group process by channeling the discussion into a relevant area.
(c) False. John's feedback was negative and thereby hindered group action.
(d) excessive length; irrelevance
(e) He gave personal encouragement to Roger and expanded Roger's ideas.
(f) False. Harry's response was neither a part of a complete feedback cycle nor clarifying in nature. It was an initial statement of warning to the group.
(g) The cycle was not complete, because Harry did not have a chance to react to Wayne's response. Thus the discussion remains an interaction and not a complete feedback cycle.
(h) The strength of Wayne's personal attack on and irrelevant threat to Harry served to anger and confuse the group to the point that group discussion was disrupted.

5. Discussion involves a group of people interacting together. Factors contributing to group identity—people feeling they are part of a group—include interdependence, common purpose, free interaction, a manageable number of participants, and an openness to one another's ideas. Which of the following situations best illustrates the factors contributing to group identity? Explain.

(a) Joe is one of several people riding an elevator in an office building. Joe says, "Sure is a nice day. Wonder how the campaign is going?" Met with silence and cold stares from those around him, Joe sheepishly retires to his own thoughts about what a bunch of stuffed shirts he's riding with.

(b) A tidal wave strikes the Poseidon during a New Year's Eve celebration party, capsizing the ship. The survivors face critical decisions. Should they remain in the ballroom, now deep in the ocean, or climb upward to gamble for survival via a possible above-water exit in the hull of the sinking ship? Before decisions are made, interaction from everyone is sought for ideas on how to circumvent each barrier along the escape route.*

- - - - - - - - - - - - - - - - - -

_____

*This selection is a description of a situation from the movie The Poseidon Adventure, courtesy Twentieth Century Fox.

(b)   This group of people seems to show all the characteristics of group identity: interdependence, common purpose, free interaction, a manageable number of participants, and an openness to one another's ideas.

6.   (a) In your own words, define discussion.

(b)   What is the importance of feedback to group discussion?

- - - - - - - - - - - - - - - - - -

(a)   Discussion is a serious sharing of information designed to help solve a
      specific problem; it is a communication process involving a group of
      people, usually under the direction of a leader, who are working toward
      a solution to a problem.
(b)   Feedback helps people adjust their messages in response to one another
      for maximum group effectiveness, with people modifying their responses
      to stimuli, both verbal and nonverbal, in a continuing cycle.

KINDS OF GROUPS

7.   All of us probably have memories of a teacher who held us after class to
"discuss" our classwork or a supervisor who called us into his or her office
to "discuss" our job performance. Often such discussions are one-sided criticisms of work or behavior, offering little in the way of mutual problem solving. Problem-solving groups differ from other collections of people labeled
as groups in that problem-solving group discussion involves decision making.
Decision-making groups have purposes apart from the social, emotional, or
self-enrichment needs of the membership. The term "discussion" implies
more than just talk among group members, nor does it mean a public address
to the membership. Discussion involves sharing, participating, and interacting in a group context.
    Sharing, participating, and interacting are not three independent elements;
instead, they overlap and function together to produce a positive backdrop for
successful group decision making. Discussion includes a common goal using
the knowledge, experience, insight, and labor of all group members (sharing);
a number of persons freely exchanging ideas (participation); and all engaged
in a face-to-face, communicative exchange (interaction). Discussion differs
from a public speaking event, for example. A public speaker may share ideas
with the audience, but the audience members will have difficulty sharing their
ideas with the speaker. Formal speeches are not designed to encourage sharing, participation, or interaction.
    Read the following case, and answer the question which follows it.

Case

As the dishes were being removed from the executive dining room, Bryan
Goodfellow, president of Goodfellow's Manufacturing and Design Company,
called the meeting to order. Customarily, the Goodfellow's president meets
during lunch with the management staff to discuss management decisions, production goals, and sales. The meetings are held monthly in the executive dining room.

Having established order, Goodfellow reviewed the past month's production
and sales figures. "Sales in Region Four are down 11 percent, while sales in
Region Six are up 9 percent...," he commented. Goodfellow steadily read
his report for nearly twenty minutes without interruption. The review finished,
Goodfellow introduced Herb Peabody, the production analyst, who informed
each department of the production goals for the next month.

As Peabody finished his report, Goodfellow thanked him for his usual close
attention to detail. Goodfellow then revealed to the staff his decision to concentrate on overseas markets to offset the "softness" in domestic sales. "I know
that this decision to concentrate on foreign markets will require extra effort
on your part," he said, "but I have confidence that our management staff can
rise to the occasion." Goodfellow brought the meeting to a close by saying,
"I see that once again we've used every bit of our scheduled meeting time, but
if any of you have questions or ideas for my consideration, please send me a
memo, and we'll discuss your ideas at the next monthly meeting."

Would you classify the case above as a problem-solving group discussion?
Explain.

- - - - - - - - - - - - - - - - - -

No. The monthly meeting at Goodfellow's would not be considered a problem-
solving group discussion. While a group of people are meeting face-to-face,
the basic elements of discussion are lacking. We observe very little sharing
of ideas; the participation is limited to the president and one other person; and
interaction is limited to almost a one-way conversation between the president
and his staff.

8.   Read the following case; and determine if it contains the basic elements of
a discussion:

Case

Bill, John, Tom, and Judith are salespeople for a local automobile dealership.
During the past three months sales have dropped 15 percent; and they decide
to meet to discuss what can be done to increase sales.

Bill, the sales manager, looked at each of the other salespeople and then
said, "You may think that I work only for Mr. Tubbs, our boss, but in a sense
I also work for all the people associated with this dealership. We have a problem which affects all of us."

John, Tom, and Judith voiced agreement. "My volume has been about the same as last year," remarked Tom, "but I've had to come in on my day off to keep it that way."

"Yeah," snipped Judith. "When you come in on your day off my sales are undercut."

"Wait just a minute," said John, as he leaned between Tom and Judith. "I remember when sales were great and we all came in on our days off, and we still couldn't spend as much time with customers as we wanted to, so let's not get on each other."

"I agree with John," said Bill. "We all want to make a living, but we've got to focus on the overall problem."

"Can we do anything about our ad campaign?" Judith asked. "I feel that it's not doing the job for us."

"Sure," Bill answered. "We can discuss any aspect of the dealership, and our advertising is a good place to start."

Would you classify the above example as problem-solving group discussion? Explain.

- - - - - - - - - - - - - - - - - -

Yes. While this is only a brief excerpt, we observe a group sharing ideas and opinions about a common problem. Also, every member participates, with interaction among them.

9. In frame 7, the Goodfellow group served mainly as an audience. The management staff at Goodfellow's makes no decisions as a group, nor do they solve problems within the context of monthly management meetings. The basic elements of discussion, as we define it, are not present. The underlying reason for using problem-solving group discussion is to bring people together so they can make mutual decisions and accomplish whatever task confronts the group. This mutual interdependence inherent in group problem-solving cannot truly exist without discussion.

If you were evaluating whether an activity uses discussion as a method, what three basic elements would you look for?

- - - - - - - - - - - - - - - - - -

sharing, participation, interaction

10. We could quite easily suggest that a group discussion be used anytime a problem exists to be solved, an issue must be studied, or a conflict must be resolved. However, group discussion is a tool; it is neither an instant remedy nor a cure-all. A group discussion will not guarantee solutions, but it will bring people together so that they may try to reach a solution.

Some critics of group discussion say, "Why bother with groups when we ought to be helping individuals to be better problem solvers?" Granted, many individuals could improve their probelm-solving abilities, but as members of society, we all face similar problems. An individual may be able to solve his or her own problems, but our common problems—whether they are related to job, school, church, or community—can best be solved through cooperative effort. For example, Tom (in frame 8) solved his personal problem of declining sales by working on his day off; however, this did not solve the dealership's problem, and it may have increased the problems of his co-workers.

Acting alone, an individual solves a problem solely on the basis of his or her knowledge and experience (even if he or she consults another), assumes whatever labor and responsibility is required, and then carries out the decision. For example, suppose that you receive a large income tax refund. Do you spend it on fun and recreation, purchase a new color TV, pay debts, or invest the money? The decision is your own, and you act independently. When a group makes a decision, the group acts upon the knowledge and experience of all its members. Through discussion, individual ideas can be challenged, strengthened, and improved before the decision is enacted. In addition, labor and responsibility are shared among the group members, which eases individual burdens and strengthens the overall commitment to the decision. In these ways, group problem-solving discussion focuses and makes better use of human resources.

Case

The governor of Montana recently ordered all state institutions to reduce energy consumption by 20 percent. The administration at one state college decided to use a group approach in conforming to the governor's order. Instead of calling the director of the physical plant and telling him to turn off the lights and reduce the heat, a committee representing a broad cross section of the campus community was formed and asked to study the problem and find solutions. The group included administrators, faculty, physical plant staff, and students. The group not only found a greater variety of energy-saving measures, but its members also shared a greater sense of involvement and enthusiasm. The campus community willingly supported the decisions of the energy group—much more than they would have supported a decree by the governor or an order by the college president.

Which of the following statements best describes the use of problem-solving group discussion?

_____ (a) Problem-solving discussion should be used any time a problem needs solving.

_____ (b) Problem-solving discussion is a sure-fire method of problem solving.

_____ (c) Problem-solving discussion is a tool through which people come together and attempt to solve problems.

- - - - - - - - - - - - - - - - - -

(c) Problem-solving discussion is a tool.

11. An individual attempting to solve a problem works alone. How does group problem solving differ?

- - - - - - - - - - - - - - - - - -

Labor is shared by the group members.

12. Compare a situation where one person is working independently to solve a problem with a situation where five people are, as a group, concentrating their efforts to solve a problem. Potentially, which situation can make better use of the people's problem-solving efforts?

- - - - - - - - - - - - - - - - -

Group problem-solving discussion makes better use of the human resources of the people. Discussion focuses those resources. Discussion involves sharing, participation, and interaction, all of which are necessary if the group's full potential is to be realized.

13. Visualize a situation in which one person makes a decision affecting a large group of people and a situation where a smaller group representing the large one makes that decision. How will people most likely respond to the small-group decision as compared to the individual decision?

- - - - - - - - - - - - - - - - -

Usually, more enthusiasm and support is generated for decisions mutually agreed upon by a group representing those affected.

14. An additional difference between individual and group decision making has to do with the membership or makeup of the group. What potential does a problem-solving group have which is not possible when only one person is involved in the decision?

- - - - - - - - - - - - - - - -

The group can broaden or spread out its membership, as in the energy example, when faculty, students, physical plant staff, and administrators were all involved in the decision making.

15. Critics of problem-solving group discussion sometimes charge that since discussion involves a number of people, groups often require more time to

reach a decision than do individuals. It does take time to hear one another out, to test ideas, and to reach agreement and consensus. However, speed and quality are not the same. The goal of group problem-solving discussion is to combine many talents and skills so that a quality solution will be reached— not necessarily a fast one. Some situations do require a speedy decision, but these are the exception. Most problems would be better solved by quality solutions than by fast solutions.

Emergency decisions, without question, require fast action. An airline pilot, forced to make a split-second, emergency decision, cannot call upon a problem-solving discussion. A paramedic arriving upon the scene of an accident must act quickly to prevent loss of life—again time does not permit discussion. We are not, however, faced with life-and-death decisions through the course of our daily activity. Questions about slumping sales, traffic congestion, unemployment, inefficient government, worker morale, energy conservation, and why Johnny can't read did not develop over night and do not require over night solution. Such problems do require good, quality solutions.

Read the following cases, and answers the question which follows them.

Case 1

Allen Kerr kept busy all night tracking the storm front on his radar scope and monitoring the weather service telex. All the conditions indicated a severe storm and a strong possibility of flash floods. A decision to issue a severe storm warning would have to be made soon. A delay might reduce the time available to evacuate low, flood-prone areas. However, Allen also realized that a false warning would unnecessarily disrupt the public and cause a costly call-up of city and county emergency personnel.

Case 2

The storm hit the city and county at 11:30 p.m. Parts of the city received fourteen inches of rain in less than one hour. Many small rivers and streams jumped their banks and covered low-lying areas with up to five feet of water. In spite of adequate warnings, some citizens ignored the emergency situation and failed to take prudent measures. For some unknown reason, the south part of the county did not hear the warning sirens. A communications breakdown delayed one fire-rescue squad in reaching a group of persons caught in an underground parking garage. The city's receiving hospital lost power for nearly thirty minutes when a backup emergency generator failed to engage. Property loss was high, and personal injuries were many. The following day, an editorial in the city paper demanded to know what the city and county governments planned to do in the future to avoid a repeat of the previous night's folly.

Analyze the interrelated problems described in cases 1 and 2. Indicate the type of decision making and problem solving appropriate in each case. Which case requires an individual and speedy decision, and which calls for thoughtful study by a group?

- - - - - - - - - - - - - - - - - -

In case 1, a speedy, individual decision seems best. The storm is building quickly, and the meteorologist must warn the population to avert loss of life. In case 2, a careful study needs to be conducted to discover why the city and county responded so poorly to the storm. Such a study would lead to a comprehensive plan of action to deal with future natural disasters. A broad-based group should be formed to study and solve the problem.

PUBLIC AND PRIVATE DISCUSSION

16. We can classify discussion groups into two categories: public and private. The difference between public and private discussion groups has little to do with the membership but a great deal to do with the structure and function of the groups. For example, meetings of private citizens are not necessarily private discussions, while public officials do not necessarily form public groups.

A private discussion group exists for the purpose of satisfying a shared need or finding a solution for a problem that is of mutual importance to the members of the group. Such discussion groups are labeled private since they usually meet and conduct their business in private. Observers may occasionally watch or monitor a private discussion group, but an audience, in the usual sense, is never present.

In contrast, a public discussion group generally meets in the presence of an audience, and the discussion functions for the benefit or enlightenment of the audience. Private discussions are marked by decision making and problem solving, while public discussion groups present information either to prepare for a decision by the larger group (the audience) or to explain a decision to the audience. In some cases, a public discussion may be used to stimulate interest in issues without regard to any particular decision.

A group of clothing buyers for a chain of department stores meets to decide what style trends and clothing lines will be featured in the stores. Would this group be considered a private or a public discussion group?

_____

- - - - - - - - - - - - - - - - - -

Private. A job-related task group meets to make a decision.

17. A conference committee of the PTA, the school board, and the Community Teachers' Association meets in the high school auditorium to discuss and answer questions about the school bond issue to be on the next election ballot. Would this meeting be considered a private or public discussion?

_____

- - - - - - - - - - - - - - - - -

Public.   The decision to have the bond election has been made.   The decision
concerning its passage is yet to be made—thus the discussion to inform the
public about the reasons for the proposed bond issue.

18. The city council holds its meetings in the civic center so that any interested citizen may come and observe the workings of city government.   At a
typical meeting, from two to four city ordinances are proposed, discussed,
and approved.   Would this be considered a private or public discussion group?

_____

- - - - - - - - - - - - - - - - -

Essentially private.   It is, however, a hybrid form of discussion, because,
although an audience may be present, decisions are made and problems solved.

19. While private discussion groups exist to satisfy a need or solve a problem
confronting the membership, a private discussion may have an extended membership.   By extended membership we are referring to other individuals who
have a stake in or who are affected by the group's decisions.   In the automobile
dealership example in frame 8, the salespeople could make decisions which
would affect the office staff, the service department, and the owner of the
dealership.   One type of private discussion group that always has an extended
membership is the committee.
    Committees tend to be formalized extensions of a larger group or organi-
zation.   In addition, membership on committees is often determined by appointment or regular work assignments.   For example, a personnel director may
serve on an employee grievance committee as a regular part of the job.   One
need only look at businesses, industries, governments, schools, or churches
to observe the pervasive use of committees as private problem-solving discussion groups.

    Why is a committee said to have extended membership?

- - - - - - - - - - - - - - - - -

Because it serves a larger group or organization.

20. Some writers on group decision making attempt to make a rigid distinction
between public and private discussion groups.   They often regard private
groups as spontaneously generated; that is, a variety of factors spontaneously
falls into place and the group emerges.   This "spontaneous generation" view
of group emergence is reminiscent of the old Andy Hardy movies where a
hodgepodge of kids suddenly realizes that some worthy cause needs money,

and Andy says, "I know how we can get the money. Let's put on a show!" The rest of the movie shows a once disorganized collection of school kids as a highly cohesive task group producing a show which would rival the best of Broadway.

While a number of factors inherent to the group process must gel in order to produce a cohesive group, in practice, groups don't usually form spontaneously. Characteristically, private problem-solving discussion groups form as an outgrowth of associations made in work, school, recreational, civic, or religious organization. Group structure and organization also need to be flexible and adaptable to meet changing situations.

The following case depicts a group which undergoes several changes through the course of its existence. Read through the case, and answer the questions that follow.

Case
In California, pollution is an extremely serious problem. Air pollution has proven to be a special physical and psychological irritant to the population. Recognizing the problem, citizens demanded that the state government take definite action to reduce the hazards associated with air pollution. Finally, the state decided to appoint a committee to investigate the problem of air pollution and to suggest specific methods for solving the problem. The governor appointed eight individuals to serve on the committee. They were instructed to report their findings to the California state legislature.

(a) How were the members of the group described above selected?

(b) Would the group described above be considered as a public or private

discussion group? _____

(c) In relation to problem-solving groups, the California state legislature represents what kind of membership? _____

- - - - - - - - - - - - - - - - - - -

(a) appointed; (b) private; (c) extended

21. Although the pollution study committee discussed in frame 20 indirectly serves the public, its members do not discuss the problem in the presence of a public audience. As a private, problem-solving discussion group, the pollution study committee served what kind of function?

- - - - - - - - - - - - - - - - - -

a decision-making or task function

22. Let's assume that the California state legislature accepts the recommendation of the pollution study committee and then directs the committee to inform the people of the state of their findings and proposed solutions. At this

point, the private discussion will become what type of discussion group?

_____

- - - - - - - - - - - - - - - - - -

public discussion group

23. Public discussion groups are not normally considered problem-solving or decision-making groups, but they do serve useful functions as providers of information, stimulators of public opinion, or consolidators of public support. Public discussion groups come in a variety of forms, but the three most common forms of public discussion groups are the panel, the symposium, and the forum. If you are either organizing or serving on a public discussion group, you will find it helpful to know the basic characteristics of each of the three types.

   A panel discussion is essentially a group of individuals (the panel) who discuss a topic for the benefit of a listening audience. Panels may be highly structured or very informal. A structured panel may limit the length and scope of remarks, while an informal panel may emphasize freewheeling, spontaneous interaction. Panel members are expected to prepare in advance for extemporaneous speaking and to have some knowledge or expertise as the basis for their comments, but formal speeches or long, prepared remarks are discouraged. Depending upon the discussion topic, a panel's membership may consist of experts or interested lay people or both. A basic criteria for a good panel discussion is interaction among the members of the panel. Through interaction, a variety of positions and ideas should be expressed, thus providing the audience with useful information. Panels usually have a moderator who guides the flow of the discussion and encourages participation from all panel members.

(a) What does panel discussion consist of?

(b) What kinds of individuals may serve on a panel?

(c) In terms of preparation, what is expected of a panel member?

(d) What is the ideal type of communication behavior for a panel discussion?

- - - - - - - - - - - - - - - - - -

(a) A group of individuals who discuss a topic for the benefit of an audience.
(b) Experts, laypeople, or both.
(c) Panel members are expected to prepare for extemporaneous discussion but not to prepare formal speeches.
(d) Spontaneous interaction among the group members.

24. A symposium consists of a group of individuals, each of whom presents a formal, prepared speech on a specific aspect or part of the discussion topic. For example, one member might present the history of a problem, while

another presents recent trends, followed by a third who presents methods of solving the problem. An alternate form of symposium might have five speakers, each presenting a different solution to a problem. Symposiums tend to be very formal and so much like a public-speaking event that some group writers discount their use as public discussions. Members of a symposium do not usually interact with one another, as do panel members, although some symposiums evolve into a panel format after the speeches are presented. Both panel discussions and symposiums are presented to an audience. An interesting variation of the symposium involves division of the audience into small discussion groups following the presentation of the symposium speeches. In this way, the symposium acts as stimulus for audience involvement.

What are the two major differences between the panel discussion format and the symposium format?

- - - - - - - - - - - - - - - - - - - -

A panel involves informal conversation between the members. Panel members are prepared but speak extemporaneously, while members of a symposium present set speeches. Interaction is encouraged in a panel but discouraged in a symposium.

In a panel discussion, members are free to discuss any area of the topic, while in a symposium each member is confined to a specific part of the topic.

25. Forum discussions involve a large group or audience which interacts and discusses as the result of some other activity. Town hall meetings, public hearings, and open city council meetings are often forums to gather public opinion or to hear citizen complaints. Often, due to large numbers of people, forums seem disorganized and rambling, but they do serve a useful purpose in encouraging citizen involvement. One kind of forum, often used on college campuses, starts with two or more speakers who deliver to a listening audience short position statements on opposing sides of an issue. Time may also be set aside after a panel or symposium discussion, using a forum approach to allow the audience to ask questions or offer opinions. After the speeches, a forum is opened to the audience, which discusses various aspects of the topic for a predetermined length of time. After the forum discussion, the audience votes, and a decision is made. Lack of adequate time is the main problem related to the forum discussion. Organizers often fail to allow enough time following the stimulus material (panel, symposium, or lecture, for example) for an adequate forum.

(a) What is the primary purpose of a forum discussion?

(b) What is the main shortcoming of most forum discussions?

- - - - - - - - - - - - - - - - - - -

(a)   To involve the audience in the discussion.

(b)   Often not enough time is set aside for the forum discussion.

26. Unfortunately, no clear-cut guidelines may be applied in determining which type of public discussion—a panel, a symposium, or a forum—best suits a given situation. Panel discussions tend to be more free-flowing and interesting to watch. Symposiums have the advantage of covering specific areas of the topic in a highly organized, precise manner. Forums tend to be less organized than symposiums, but they do have the advantage of involving the audience directly in the proceedings.

Each of the following cases describes a type of public discussion. Read the cases, and identify the type of discussion.

Case 1

West-central Missouri lies over several proven coal deposits which have been partially mined for over sixty years. Large-scale mining has been limited to a few concentrated areas due to the value of the farmland above the coal and the easy access to better-quality coal elsewhere in the nation. However, the energy crisis has sparked new interest in the coal lying beneath the surface of West-central Missouri. Along with the new interest has come the question of industrial development versus environmental protection. In order to better inform the public of the issues involved in coal mining, a local state university made time available on its public broadcasting channel for a public discussion. Five individuals representing different views on the subject were invited: Mr. James Haslid of Peabody Coal, area mining operations chief; Dr. Elizabeth Conners of the university, associate professor of earth science; The Hon. David Wright, representing the 35th district in the state senate; Mr. Harry Miller, State Department of Natural Resources; and Fr. Earl Gibbons of Faith Episcopal Church, chairman of Citizens for a Clean Environment.

The members of the discussion were seated in a semicircle facing a studio audience. The program host first asked them to introduce themselves, after which any member might begin the discussion by addressing the topic "Energy and Environment: Can Missouri Have Both?"

(a)   Is the public discussion above a forum, a symposium, or a panel?

_____

Case 2

Disappointment in the quality of education, charges of mismanaged school funds, and a school superintendent generally perceived as inept lead five candidates to file for the single opening on the district school board. The local League of Women Voters was both delighted and concerned by the turn of events. The League saw the large number of candidates as a sign of widespread public involvement but felt that the number of candidates might confuse the voters and make their selection difficult. The League proposed that a public discussion be held in which all five candidates would be allowed equal time to present their views on the school system and public education.

A large crowd arrived at the high school auditorium to hear the candidates discuss the coming election. Since two of the candidates stated that they would not engage in a debate, the following ground rules governed the duscussion: Each candidate would be allowed eight minutes to present his or her views; no candidate might interrupt another during the allotted eight minutes; and no exchanges between candidates were allowed between presentations.

(b) What type of public discussion is the above—a forum, a symposium, or a

  panel? _____

Case 3
A "tempest in a teapot" developed in the city when the city manager proposed that the private, independent trash haulers be replaced by a citywide municipal system. The six private trash haulers, who had never before agreed on the time of day, united to petition the city council. Citizen complaints poured into city hall, while the local paper carried angry letters to the editor. Sensing a political backlash, the city council announced that the topic would be discussed at its next meeting.

An overflow crowd greeted the council as it arrived at city hall. People were packed shoulder-to-shoulder, with many persons lining the stairway and hall leading to the councilroom. A few "Save Free Enterprise—Fire the Manager" signs were visible, but the crowd on the whole behaved in a polite, orderly fashion.

After the routine business was finished, councilman William Hull addressed the mayor and moved that the remainder of the session be devoted to the trash issue, and that the meeting reconvene in the civic building where all could be seated. The motion passed.

At the civic building, the mayor announced that the council would rather hear the feelings and opinions of the public than debate the issue; therefore the meeting was opened to anyone who wanted to discuss the issue of public versus municipal trash collection. A cloud of hands rose.

(c) What kind of public discussion is the above—a forum, a symposium, or a

  panel? _____

- - - - - - - - - - - - - - - - - - - -

(a) a panel; (b) a symposium; (c) a forum

GROUP ECOLOGY

27. We cannot study group discussion without examining certain physical elements that affect the group. These elements—group size, meeting facilities, and room arrangement—combine to form what we call group ecology. The ecology of a group can play an important part in determining the group's structure, interaction, and, therefore, results.

First, we must consider how many people are necessary to compose a group. Essentially, a group means more than one person, but beyond that, the size of a group is determined by its purpose. If the group's purpose includes encouraging individual input, a small group may be desirable. If the group's purpose is to expose members to a variety of viewpoints, a larger group is better. The group should be large enough so that all the task-oriented and people-oriented skills (which we will discuss later) necessary for accomplishment of the job are represented in the group.

Five to seven participants is generally a comfortable size for a work group, so the group is neither too small to share a task nor too large to prevent everyone from sharing their ideas with one another. Groups with more than five to seven members may promote the birth of subgroups, because it is hard for everyone to have a chance to share their ideas. An odd number of members may be preferable, because a majority position will most likely result when a vote is taken. Disagreements are not necessarily unhealthy, but a majority result can overcome the frustration of an impasse when a vote is taken.

A second area of group ecology that we must consider is the meeting facilities. Research has shown that environmental surroundings have a direct influence on group behavior. The size, decoration, lighting, and cleanliness of the meeting room can affect the attitudes and feelings of the group members. Rooms that are tastefully decorated, indirectly lit, arranged in a neat, orderly fashion, and sized adequately to house the group tend to facilitate the discussion process. Conversely, rooms that are ugly, harshly lit, dirty, disorderly, and too big or too small tend to inhibit the group discussion process.

If you have no choice about room size and decoration for your group, you can still do several things to improve the environment. If the room is too large, you can rearrange portable dividers, blackboards, and other furniture to make the room appear smaller. Arranging the tables, chairs, and other furniture in a neat, orderly way can also make a room more attractive. Simply arranging notebooks, pens, and ashtrays in front of each chair at the table can add a positive note to the environment.

Being face-to-face in discussion adds both to the feeling of group identity and to the communication process. For maximum interaction, therefore, group members need to be able to see one another. The third element of group ecology, then, is the seating arrangement. For maximum efficiency, the group should be seated close enough together so they can speak to one another at a comfortable volume. This close arrangement facilitates not only verbal communication but also the messages sent through actions and expression (nonverbal communication).

Research indicates that nonverbal communication plays a vital role in our total communication efforts. While we will not examine nonverbal communication in detail, a cursory review of some aspects of it will be useful at this point.

One important aspect of nonverbal behavior is facial expression. Often we can determine emotional states, attitudes, and reactions to the comments of others by watching the facial expressions of group members. Thus we can tell whether our messages are being understood, how they are being received, and if we need to defend our statements, simply by observing the facial reactions of our fellow group members. Note, however, that members of our society often attempt to mask or disguise feelings and reactions. Therefore, facial expression is not a foolproof indicator of what a person is actually thinking or feeling.

A second aspect of nonverbal communication, related to room arrangement, is territoriality. Territoriality can be defined as a feeling of "controlling rights" over a certain geographical area when no legal ownership right to that area has been established. For example, if you sit in the same place at every meeting of a group, you tend to think that that place is "yours." Territoriality can play an important role in the group discussion process. If one person's territory is violated by someone else, attitudes and feelings may become strained or even hostile within the group, causing the discussion process to break down. On the other hand, if careful attention is paid to the "territory" of others, the group discussion process can be aided.

Closely related to the concept of territoriality is that of personal space, which refers to the distance you place between yourself and others. This distance, which varies from situation to situation and person to person, is seldom noticed until it is violated. Then the person whose space has been violated may become defensive or hostile or even move away from the interpersonal contact. Group members need to be aware of personal space if they want to keep group relations functioning smoothly.

Because some seating arrangements are conducive to verbal and nonverbal interaction and some are not, you should carefully plan the seating arrangement for any problem-solving discussion. A circular arrangement often best accomplishes the goals of most discussion groups. This arrangement brings everyone as close together as is possible and desirable in an equally face-to-face position. The circle also tends to reduce superior positions which may be present with a semi-circular, rectangular, linear, or other geometric arrangement. Obviously a circular pattern would be less than desirable for a public forum or symposium. Circular arrangements are best for private or closed meetings where no audience is present.

But suppose you inherit a square or rectangular table. What can you do to promote interaction? You can encourage those seated at the middle portion of the longer sides of a rectangle to push their chairs out from the table to form more of an oval pattern. With square tables, you might consider placing several small tables together to form an oval or circular pattern. A bit of creative thinking can help you overcome apparent barriers. Recently a hexagon-shaped table (see figure 1 at the top of the next page) has grown in popularity. It seems to satisfy the compromise when a group has neither the room for nor availability of a round table.

The seating behavior of group participants also has implications for the group discussion process. The table positions assumed by the group members often indicate the roles the members play in the group—or the roles they may play. Research indicates that the person who sits at the head of a rectangular or hexagon-shaped table tends to be the leader of the group or to have a better opportunity to emerge as leader.

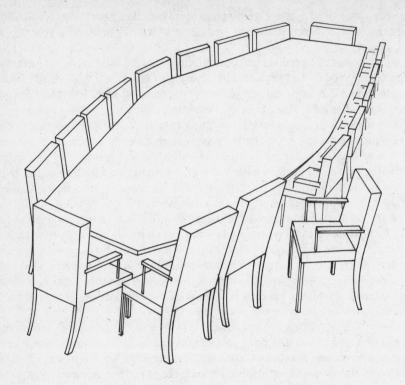

Figure 1. Hexagon-shaped table.

It is not clear whether the seating position makes the leader, or the potential leader chooses a position he or she feels to have a greater source of influence. In Chapter 6, we will discuss leadership emergence.

Just as some positions are more conducive to leadership, some seating positions are more suited to passive roles. People occupying positions B and D in Figure 2 tend to play passive roles, while those occupying A, C, and E tend to assume dominant roles with either A or E most likely to emerge as

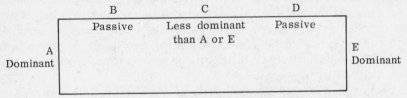

Figure 2. Seating chart showing
dominant and passive positions.

leader. Again research has not yet clarified whether the position or the person makes the difference in the interaction.

Groups can successfully engage in problem-solving discussion without being face-to-face. A standard example is the conference telephone call often used in the business world. However, such an example is the exception, not the rule. And such groups can be severely handicapped unless the participants know one another well enough to share freely their feelings and doubts in the decision-making process. In face-to-face encounters, we can move cautiously into controversial areas by "testing the waters" through monitoring nonverbal messages of approval or disapproval when we are unsure of the reactions of other group members. Furthermore, in face-to-face encounters we can better confirm that the thread of conversation is being processed by each listener as we share our thoughts with one another. We can tell from others' reactions what areas need more explanation and what is understood; on the basis of this feedback we can adjust our messages. Thus communication should improve.

We have seen that room size, facilities, and arrangements can play a vital role in the group process. Read and compare the following cases. The questions that follow them will help you test how well you understand the principles of group ecology.

Case 1

The uptown Optimist Club executive council meets once a month in the conference/banquet room of a local restaurant. The restaurant has a policy of arranging the facilities of the banquet room to meet the needs of the various groups using the room. This banquet room is carpeted and painted in soft, warm colors, and lit with indirect fluorescent tubes and direct decorative fixtures. The room is so constructed as to allow for variety in furniture placement and room size through the use of movable partitions.

The president of the Optimist Club always arranges to have the room sized to hold five men at a rectangular table. According to the president's specifications, note pads, pens, ash trays, typed agendas, and all other needed items are neatly arranged at each seat. The seating positions are in keeping with the diagram in Figure 3.

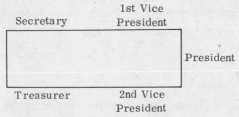

Figure 3. Seating arrangement for
Optimist Club executive council.

Case 2

The monthly meeting of the County Historical Society is held in the town meeting hall. The society has no chairman, so no one makes advance arrangements to structure the meeting room in any particular fashion. The town meeting hall is designed to hold five hundred people in rows of movable folding chairs facing a large raised platform at one end of the room. When the eight members of the society arrive, they find the meeting hall dark, so one of the members turns on all of the direct overhead lights. The group arranges itself across the front row of chairs.

(a) Which group members may be expected to leave the meeting with better attitudes and a greater feeling of accomplishment? Why?

(b) What one thing could the Optimist Club do to facilitate more face-to-face interaction?

(c) What could the County Historical Society do to make the best of their facilities?

(d) Do the seating positions of the Optimist Club have any significance?

(e) Is there any distinct indication of who may emerge as leader in the County Historical Society?

(f) Which group has the best potential to observe and react to facial expressions of the group members?

(g) What are some possible problems with the size of the County Historical Society?

(h) Which group has the greatest potential for territorial violations?

- - - - - - - - - - - - - - - - - - - -

(a) The Optimist Club discussed in Case 1. The room arrangement is more conducive to a positive attitude toward the group and facilitates the group process.

(b) They could arrange for a circular table.

(c) They could arrange their chairs in a circle. If they wanted to be innovative, they could de-emphasize the size of the room by lighting only the portion they were using or by moving the group to the platform.

(d) Yes, the president has placed himself in a leadership position. Since only two people sit on either side of the table, each of the other four men are in similar active/passive role positions.

(e) Probably not. As long as the groups stay in a linear arrangement, total group interaction may not be great enough to allow one person to emerge as leader.

(f) The Optimist Club. This situation is the better of the two, but it could be improved at a circular table.

(g) The group is large enough that it might break up into subgroups, especially with their seating arrangement. Also, the even number of members in this group may, at times, make it difficult to obtain a majority opinion.

(h) The County Historical Society. Since this group has no assigned seating arrangement, informal territory may be assumed after several meetings. Since the Optimist Club group has assigned seats, each member knows beforehand what his position will be.

SUMMARY

In this chapter we have discussed the nature of problem-solving discussion as a communication process involving a group of people, usually under the direction of a leader, working toward a solution to a problem. We noted that free interaction, interdependence, manageable size, and openness to one another's ideas all contribute to building group identity. We also distinguished between private and public discussions; contrasted panels, symposiums, and forums; and compared the merits of individual and group decision making. Finally, we pointed out how ecological factors play a vital role in facilitating the discussion process.

SELF-TEST

The following questions will help you assess how well you understand the material in Chapter 1. Answer the questions, and then look at the answers and review instructions that follow.

1. Define discussion.

2. Explain the importance to group discussion of (a) feedback and (b) group identity.

3. When is it generally best for one person to make a decision? When do group decisions tend to be best?

4. Distinguish between public and private discussion.

5. Briefly characterize the most common formats for public discussions.

6. What common ecological factors have an impact on discussion? Explain.

Answers to Self-Test

Compare your answers to the questions on the Self-Test with the answers given below. If all your answers are correct, go on to the next chapter. If you had difficulty with any questions, you may want to review the frames indicated in parentheses following the answer. If you missed several questions, you should probably reread the entire chapter carefully.

1. Discussion is a serious sharing of information designed to help solve a specific problem; it is a communication process involving a group of people, usually under the direction of a leader, who are working toward a solution to a problem. (frames 1-6)

2. (a) Feedback facilitates message adjustments for maximum group effectiveness. It is a cycle of responses to stimuli, both verbal and nonverbal, with people modifying their responses in reaction to others. The resulting

mutual influence is central to real group interaction.

(b) Discussion also thrives best where a group identity prevails. Group identity is nurtured through interdependence, common purpose, free interaction, a manageable number of participants, an openness to one another's ideas, and a sense of sharing, participating, and interacting together. (frames 4-6)

3. While individual decision can be as effective as, and sometimes superior to, group decisions, group decisions generally are superior because they draw on the resources of a number of people. In an emergency situation where time is at a premium, an individual decision, made by one well-informed person who is able to think clearly under adverse conditions, might be best. When time is not a premium and the problem is complex, a pooling of ideas by a group should generally yield a better solution, and the group is more likely to support a decision they have helped form. (frames 7-15)

4. A private discussion group exists to satisfy a shared need or to find a solution for a mutually recognized problem. A traditional audience is never present for this type of discussion. In contrast, a public discussion group generally meets in the presence of an audience, and its function is primarily educational. (frames 16-22)

5. The main formats used in public discussion are the panel, the symposium, and the forum. The panel format tends to be informal and spontaneous in interaction patterns, while the symposium is much more formal, with members presenting prepared speeches which address some dimension of an issue. In the forum, however, the audience becomes the stimulus for interaction through questions they address to panel or symposium members. (frames 23-26)

6. (a) Size. The group should be large enough to accomplish its purpose, so members do not become overworked and therefore discouraged. However, groups should not be so large that they must fragment into subgroups if all are to be able to voice their ideas. Five to seven members is often a comfortable number for most work groups.

(b) Environmental factors of the meeting place are important. For example, the room size, decor, lighting, and cleanliness can have an impact on the attitudes and feelings of all participants.

(c) Face-to-face exchanges tend to enhance group identity. Therefore, seating arrangements that are conducive to eye contact and closer proximity of the members tend to stimulate interaction.

(d) Territorial rights can present a hazard and must be handled carefully to keep group relations harmonious.

(e) Seating positions can encourage or discourage interaction. So, for example, a judicious planner can encourage passive members to interact more freely by placing them in more dominant positions at the table. (frame 27)

CHAPTER TWO

Problem-Solving Discussion as a Process

In Chapter 2 we will look at problem solving as a process. A process is a sequence of ever-changing events or actions, over time, in progression toward some objective. A process has no beginning or end but suggests continuous action—like a river, ever-changing, ever-moving. The better you understand the factors influencing the discussion process, the more effectively you can help the group achieve its goals.

In Chapter 2 we will also explore some of the important factors that affect the problem-solving discussion process. We will also explore how characteristics interact with and affect one another. Our discussion will also center around the events or actions that most affect the discussion process in small groups.

OBJECTIVES

When you have completed this chapter, you will be able to:

- Explain the following concepts as they relate to the small group: process, primary tension, secondary tension, cohesiveness, productivity, and commitment.

- Describe how cohesiveness, productivity, and commitment interact to affect the small-group discussion process.

- Discuss the concept of congruence as it applies to task or process considerations in the small group.

1. If we were investigating reasons for failure among entering college freshmen, we would select freshman student characteristics suspected of bearing on failure versus success. Characteristics such as intelligence, determination, and willingness to seek help when needed would probably be among the elements we would examine. Other variables such as hair color or manner of dressing probably would be unimportant to us.

We may discover a very intelligent freshman who is flunking out of school. Our investigation may indicate that this particular student has no discipline and refuses to study. As a result, one factor (refusal to study) interacts with and affects another (high intelligence).

In small groups, variables work in the same way. Each small group involves several different, yet related, characteristics that interact with one another and influence the ongoing nature of the group. Some of these characteristics are more important than others. Particularly important are those factors that affect group productivity. If we can discover how certain interacting elements affect group productivity, perhaps we can introduce changes within the process which will lead to a more efficient and productive group. Obviously, we cannot isolate all of the interacting factors affecting the problem-solving discussion process. Each group is unique, composed of individual features not necessarily present in other groups.

(a) In your own words, define process as it applies to problem-solving discussion in a small group.

(b) Is it true or false that it is possible to isolate all the characteristics affecting the small-group process? Explain.

- - - - - - - - - - - - - - - - - - -

(a) Process is a series of interrelated events or actions, over time, in progression toward some goal or objective.
(b) False. An infinite number of factors may affect the small-group discussion process.

TENSION AND CONGRUENCE

2.   Tension ranks among the most important elements affecting the group discussion process. Within the small group are two general types of tension: primary and secondary. Primary tension is the awkward feeling of uneasiness, anxiety, or awkwardness, akin to stage fright, that we have when we first meet a stranger. It tends to manifest itself in apathy, politeness, long periods of silence, and very tentative statements such as "I'm not sure this idea has any merit but..." Such tension usually occurs as a result of our uncertainty concerning the stranger's interests, life-style, and other personal characteristics. Indeed, other people also experience primary tension as they attempt to communicate with us. Primary tension generally dissipates as people become acquainted with each other. If the tension continues, as it sometimes does, people will likely seek other relationships where no such tension is experienced.

Like individuals, small groups also experience primary tension. Often group members have not met before or share only a casual acquaintance as do two strangers who have just met. The group members experience the same feelings—the awkward moments, the feeling of anxiety, the desire to impress. Because each group is different, the degree of tension felt varies considerably from group to group. Some groups report little, if any, tension; others indicate a high degree of tension. Primary tension is a relatively normal occurrence during the first few small-group meetings; it is not destructive to the discussion process unless it becomes expected or normative behavior. If primary tension continues, the group will have serious problems in accomplishing its objectives. Let's look at a small group experiencing serious primary tension.

Case

A political science professor assigned her students to four small groups. The groups were directed to discuss and resolve problems created by reverse discrimination practices. This assignment was an extension of a unit dealing with governmental regulations regarding admission to professional schools. One of the four student groups was conspicuously quiet and inactive. Each member of the group had expressed great interest in the topic during general class discussion. When placed in the small group, however, each of the five members remained uneasily quiet. They refused to look at each other or to discuss their feelings of uneasiness. After several minutes elapsed, one group member said, "We really need to get to work on this project. Soon the professor is going to ask us about our solution." Although each member of the group nodded approval, no one replied, so the speaker responded to the group by refusing to say anything else. The time elapsed, and the group left the class. Two meetings followed, and primary tension continued to plague this small group. During the final meeting, group members began to communicate. Their communication, however, was infrequent and dealt only with irrelevant superficial matters. Finally, out of frustration, a member suggested, "Time is now critical. We must formulate some conclusions regarding the issue of reverse discrimination." One of the members countered, "Say anything you want—I really don't care."

Obviously this group was experiencing some serious problems. Let's examine and analyze these difficulties to find ways of resolving them. A casual observer might suggest that the group members are simply not interested in the topic and are therefore quiet and not involved. During earlier class discussions, however, each of the five members had appeared quite concerned and involved with the topic, and they were generally quite interested in controversial topics. Lack of interest, therefore, does not seem to explain this particular group's failure. Comments from group members provide possible reasons for this group's difficulties. One member indicated that he felt uncertian about his ideas; he was afraid other group members would disapprove of his thoughts, so he remained quiet. Two other members indicated similar fears. The final two members said that they were always followers; they did not want to be group leaders so they remained quiet. Such comments are typical from group members who have experienced primary tension and have allowed this tension to continue and become the expected or normative behavior for the group.

In this case, the five group members remained quiet due to each member's personal feelings of insecurity. Groups experiencing such tension need to delay discussing the task at hand until the primary tension problem can be resolved. In this case, a member might suggest that the group cease attempt to discuss reverse discrimination and focus on the social problem: primary tension. The member might say, "I don't think we are going to accomplish anything the way we're going. Perhaps we need to discover reasons for our lack of participation. I would like to start by discussing my fear of having ideas rejected. That's why I don't communicate." A simple acknowledgment such as this one may open the communication channels. After each member explains his or her reluctance to join the discussion, the group members can deal with their feelings. Reassurance that each member's efforts will be appreciated will facilitate effective communication.

Often, the time spent in getting to know members of your group—their names, where they are from, their hobbies, and other information which emerges from small talk—may help overcome the anxiety present in new groups. If the members are meeting for the first time, someone should make a point of seeing that everyone is introduced to the group. Once the social problem has been dealt with—once the ice has been broken—the group can return to or begin their task. Thus, primary tension is one of the important elements affecting and interacting with other aspects of the group discussion process. In the above case, primary tension adversely affected both the cohesion and the productivity of the group.

(a) What is primary tension?

(b) What are the signs of primary tension in small groups?

(c) What are some ways of overcoming primary tension in a group?

- - - - - - - - - - - - - - - - - -

(a) A feeling of uneasiness, anxiety, or awkwardness, akin to stage fright, often associated with first meeting someone.
(b) Members tend to be very polite and seem apathetic. Communication is characterized by long periods of silence and very tentative statements.
(c) Primary tension can be overcome by breaking the ice at the beginning of meetings with small talk about members' jobs and activities, especially if the group members are strangers. Additionally, members can be

reassured that their ideas are appreciated and helpful to the group. Time judiciously spent in socializing is invaluable in overcoming primary tension. If the tension persists, the group should discuss the tension and dispel the problem before attempting to continue with the task.

3.   The other type of tension occurring in small groups is called secondary tension. Secondary tension usually occurs after the primary tension has been resolved. It generally results from feelings of frustration, environmental pressures, role conflicts, and other types of interpersonal conflicts that escalate above the tolerance threshold of the group. Just as some individuals can endure more pain than others, some groups can tolerate more tension than others before they begin to dysfunction. Like primary tension, secondary tension may not occur at all, or many occur in varying degrees. The goal of group members should be to develop mechanisms for reducing tension when it rises above their endurance level. As with primary tension, secondary tension often demands a cessation of task discussion until the tension is resolved.

Secondary tensions often result from hidden agendas. Simply defined, a hidden agenda refers to a member's feelings about an issue or about another member that are not openly discussed but definitely affect the group discussion process and create secondary tension. Secondary tension also interacts with other factors that affect the problem-solving process in small groups. Let's look at a case of how secondary tension affects the small group.

Case

In a medium-sized business firm, Wayne, Allan, Fran, Ruth, and Betty form a work team that meets once a week. Before one of the group meetings, Wayne insulted Ruth in front of her boss. Ruth was very angry with Wayne but did not discuss her feelings with him. Instead, she decided to "get back at Wayne" during their next group meeting. Therefore, she came to the meeting with a hidden agenda. During the next meeting, Wayne suggested several approaches to the issues under discussion. For each suggestion, Ruth, attempting to belittle Wayne, commented that he was stupid and naive concerning the issues.

Obviously, Ruth's behavior restricted the effectiveness of the group, and the tension created caused the group to malfunction. Until Ruth and Wayne resolve their conflict, the group will waste valuable time and energy. When such tension occurs, the group should stop the discussion and deal with the tension honestly and openly. Members should see that Wayne and Ruth resolve their interpersonal conflicts so the group can return to discussing the task.

Open and honest conflict should not be confused with hidden agendas or other causes of secondary tension. Conflict in a small group generally facilitates group functioning. When an idea is presented, much conflict may exist among the members over the worth of the idea. Such conflict is healthy and should be encouraged, because it often sharpens issues, resulting in the best examination of and ultimate solution to a problem. Only when people come to the group with ulterior motives unrelated to the task is the resulting secondary tension harmful to the small-group process.

Secondary tension may also result from a role struggle between two or more members. For example, each of two members may want to be leader of the group. Instead of openly indicating their interests in leadership, they may compete with each other during group meetings. If one suggests an idea, the other feels obligated to attack it. If the two members are more concerned with their selfish interests than with the group's goals, the group suffers. Members recognizing this type of role struggle might suggest that the group appoint or elect a leader, resolving the tension regarding leadership of the group.

Other types of personality conflicts may also lead to the creation of secondary tension. For instance, if one group member is constantly belittling others, potentially active group members may become submissive for fear of being put down. Again, this situation may cause tension within the group. To resolve the tension, the group should inform the member of his or her destructive effect upon other group members. Often the person will be unaware of the problem and, once informed of the group's negative reaction, will quickly change his or her behavior. In each instance of secondary tension, the group must deal with the source of the tension openly and honestly. Most group tensions can be dealt with easily, freeing the group to move foward with the group task.

(a) What is secondary tension?

(b) Give at least two possible causes of secondary tension.

(c) When a group is experiencing primary or secondary tension, what should members do to resolve the tension?

(d) How do primary and secondary tension relate to group discussion process?

- - - - - - - - - - - - - - - - - - - -

(a) Secondary tension is a feeling of discomfort above the tolerance threshold of the group, often resulting from role conflicts, personality conflicts, hidden agendas, or environmental factors.
(b) role struggles, hidden agendas, disagreement over ideas, personality conflicts
(c) Stop discussing task-related issues and discuss the causes of the tension that is hindering the group process.
(d) Both interact with other characteristics to affect the group discussion process. Unless the group resolves the tension, the group will probably not accomplish its objectives.

4.   Look at the following cases taken from the movie Twelve Angry Men.

Case 1
Twelve men are instructed to determine the guilt or innocence of an eighteen-year-old youth accused of stabbing his father. The judge, before releasing the men from the jury box for their deliberation, admonishes them concerning the grave responsibility with which they are charged. After they are ushered into the deliberation room, they exchange considerable small talk. One juror comments to another that he is surprised that they have been locked in the room. Statements about the trial are very tentative, concerning the skill of the defense attorney. The jurors, in general, are very polite in their communication of amenities concerning the trial proceedings and their personal lives.

Case 2
The foreman instructs everyone to take his seat according to jury numbers, in chronological order. One man suggests that a preliminary vote be taken. Others support this suggestion, observing that an early vote is customary. Subsequently, the men agree to cast their votes by raising their hands if they feel the accused is guilty. Four or five hands are raised, and soon hands ripple up around the room until eleven hands attest to the jurors' belief that the boy on trial is guilty. The twelfth member votes not guilty. The onslaught of verbal and nonverbal abuse is overwhelming. One man remarks, "Boy, there's always one bleeding heart." Another man rises from his chair and paces the floor. "Why don't you throw a quarter in a collection box for underprivileged children?" he shouts to the juror who voted not guilty.

Later in the proceedings a juror notes that the boy must be guilty because of his ethnic background. Indignant at this remark, the oldest member of the deliberating body rises from his chair and exclaims that the kind of boy on trial has nothing to do with the issue confronting the group. Thereafter, tempers escalate, and most of the jurors storm away from the table incited by how prejudice has obscured truth.

Although the group finally reaches consensus, it is not without a number of hidden agendas surfacing, innumerable interpersonal conflicts, and strong disagreement over ideas. However, the problem-solving process yields a number of new insights that did not come out in the trial proceedings. These findings are invaluable in the group's quest for truth.*

(a) Which of the two cases provides an example of primary tension? Explain.

(b) Which case provides an example of secondary tension? Explain.

---

*These two selections are descriptions of situations from the television play Twelve Angry Men by Reginald Rose. Copyright © 1956 by Reginald Rose.

- - - - - - - - - - - - - - - - - - -

(a) Case 1. The jurors are polite, and their statements are very tentative since they are unsure about how others will accept their ideas.
(b) Case 2. The jurors strongly disagree over the guilt or innocence of the youth. The tension is manifested by strong verbal abuse. Furthermore, a number of hidden agendas surface, and the jurors disagree violently over ideas. The redeeming value of the whole problem-solving process, however, was that a better decision seemed to emerge as a result. Moreover, the strong conflict sharpened issues and ultimately added to the cohesion of the group.

5. Psychologist Carl Rogers offers us a unique way of examining our honesty as we interact with people in a variety of situations.* Rogers suggests that we strive for a feeling of <u>congruence</u>, which has three aspects. First, we usually have a gut reaction or internal feeling regarding important issues, situations, or people. Rogers suggests that we should not deny our feelings but rather become aware of them. Finally, we should communicate those feelings. Other communication researchers confirm that many of us repress our real feelings. Often, such repression is due to fear of being rejected by our associates. To be a freely functioning person, each participant in the small group must recognize his or her feelings and communicate them. With the resulting congruence, the communication channels will remain open, and the group will not waste energy attempting to deal with hidden agendas and other types of personality conflicts. Note that congruence does not imply being rude or abrasive to others. It simply means being honest in recognizing your feelings and communicating those feelings truthfully.

A feeling of congruence among group members allows the communication channels to remain open on the task issues as well as the social issues. As an example of congruence on the task level, let us examine some responses in a discussion about the hiring of minority groups at the Brookes Manufacturing Company. Rick, a group member, said that minority groups are generally nothing but "troublemakers" and should not be seriously considered for employment at Brookes. Harold, another group member, became angry with Rick's attitude; to be congruent, Harold must be aware of his feelings of anger and communicate them to Rick. For example, Harold might say, "What you said about minorities, Rick, really makes me feel angry." Such an honest

---

*Carl R. Rogers, "The Interpersonal Relationship: The Core of Guidance." Reprinted in <u>Bridges</u> <u>Not</u> <u>Walls</u>, 2nd ed., by John Stewart, Addison-Wesley Publishing Co., Reading, Mass. (1977), pp. 242-243.

disclosure allows Rick and Harold openly to discuss their respective positions regarding minorities. If Harold were not congruent with his feelings, his anger might adversely affect his future interactions with Rick and the rest of the group.

Group members often hesitate to be honest with others—they don't want to rock the boat. But unless you are honest, your group will arrive at final decisions that do not reflect the feelings of all group members. If this occurs, the commitment among group members is often lacking, which may prevent the effective implementation of the group's findings. Once again, the process is affected by several interacting variables.

Congruence can also affect process issues. For example, Kathy and Susan both wanted to be leader of their group. At each meeting the two fought for the leadership position. Each would try to outdo the other in every area. Jean recognized what was going on and realized how destructive the leadership fight was to the group process. She allowed Kathy and Susan's battle to continue for a couple of meetings. Finally, she realized how angry she felt. She decided to discuss her anger with Kathy and Susan. Jean approached the two and indicated that she felt angry and why. As a result, the problem was soon solved. If Jean had remained quiet, the group might never have accomplished its goal. Thus, congruence is important when dealing with both task and social issues.

What is congruence?

- - - - - - - - - - - - - - - - - -

Congruence is the recognition, acceptance, and honest expression of feelings. Rogers says that congruence involves three stages: a gut reaction, an awareness of that reaction, and communication of that reaction.

COHESIVENESS, PRODUCTIVITY, AND COMMITMENT

6.   Group cohesiveness is another important aspect of the small-group discussion process. Generally, cohesiveness is defined as a feeling of loyalty to the group. A military description might be a feeling of esprit de corps, or a feeling of all-for-one-and-one for all. A more technical definition might suggest that in a cohesive group, factors attracting members to the group are greater than factors that repel members from the group. In a highly cohesive group, members accept the goals of the group as their own. They have a strong commitment to the group and to each other, often talking in terms of "we," "us," or "our." Members of cohesive groups feel free to discuss the issues openly and to disagree with one another. Such disagreements are viewed as avenues for reaching effective decisions regarding the task of the group.

Groups experiencing high cohesiveness have usually spent some time together; cohesiveness generally does not develop overnight. Often, the cohesive group spends time in social interplay. Members are interested in one another and want to share interesting life experiences with one another. Such interplay is valuable for the creation of cohesiveness and should not be discouraged. Some observers mistakenly criticize groups for indulging in any activity other than those dealing specifically with the task. Such critics are unaware of the importance of such activity in creating a cohesive atmosphere in the small group.

A group can become highly cohesive on the social level and never complete its task. Such a situation is counterproductive. A group may also be highly cohesive regarding the task and noncohesive on the social level. Such a situation frequently occurs when groups are joined to discuss a topic of concern.

When we are in groups, we most enjoy and profit from the group that is cohesive on the social as well as the task level. Within such a group, we grow personally as well as achieving the group's goals. A group that is not cohesive is generally marked by member disinterest and lack of commitment to the group's goals.

Cohesiveness in the small-group discussion process is closely related to group productivity. In this instance, productivity simply means the completion of the task assigned to or chosen by the group. Highly cohesive groups may take longer to accomplish their task or to achieve their goals. That may surprise you. Remember, however, that members of cohesive groups feel free to disagree, argue, and thoroughly discuss every issue. Such deliberation takes time. Groups experiencing little cohesiveness often discuss the issues superficially, being more concerned with completing the project quickly than with the quality of the work. Factors that typically contribute to a noncohesive group are lingering primary tension, secondary tension, lack of interest among members, poorly defined goals, and a negative social climate.

One other variable, commitment, is important to include in a discussion of cohesiveness and productivity. Commitment is demonstrated by how much members work to put a decision into effect. Commitment is especially dramatized by the willingness of disagreeing members to accept and personally carry out the decisions of the group. Cohesiveness, commitment, and productivity closely interrelate in the problem-solving discussion process. The noncohesive group can appear more productive than the cohesive group. Because the noncohesive group generally moves much faster in its deliberation than does the cohesive group, the noncohesive group often appears to be accomplishing more—and may, in fact, be doing so. But how do the two groups compare in their commitment to their conclusions, decisions, and policies?

Generally, the cohesive group is far more committed to its final decisions than the noncohesive group. The cohesive group has argued, disagreed, agreed, and generally thoroughly investigated their topic. Such investigation most often results in a decision all group members can support, so the cohesive group is usually more committed to its findings and more willing to implement them. Since the noncohesive group does not generally investigate so thoroughly or become so involved with its topic, its members are not as committed to implementing their results. Exceptions always occur; occasionally, an uncohesive group is highly productive and committed. Generally, however, the cohesive group is more productive and committed to carrying out the group's intentions.

(a) What is group cohesiveness?

(b) What are some signs of cohesion in a group?

(c) What do we mean by productivity in a small group?

(d) What do we mean by commitment?

(e) How do cohesiveness, productivity, and commitment relate to each other?

(f) Is it true or false that a cohesive group is always more productive than a noncohesive group? _____

(g) Is it true or false that a cohesive group is generally more committed to the group's intentions than is the noncohesive group? _____

- - - - - - - - - - - - - - - - - - -

(a) A feeling of togetherness, loyalty, _esprit_ de _corps_. Factors attracting members to the group are greater than factors repelling them from the group.

(b) Cohesive groups use pronouns such as "we," "us," and "our." Cohesive groups are noisier than noncohesive groups; they feel free to disagree with one another, to challenge the decisions and actions of other group members. They have a good time and tend to be more productive than noncohesive groups, though they often take longer to conclude their deliberations.

(c) Accomplishing the group's task or goals regarding the selected or assigned task.

(d) Sufficient belief in the decisions or solutions of the group, so that each member is willing to implement the group's findings, even those who disagree with the group's decision.

(e) Cohesiveness affects the social and task levels of the group. A group that is cohesive on the task level is usually more productive and more committed to the group's intentions than is the noncohesive group. The noncohesive group may seem to be more productive in terms of specific accomplishments, but its members normally are not as committed to implementing their findings as is the cohesive group.

(f) False. A cohesive group is usually more productive than a noncohesive group, but not always.

(g) True.

7. Any group can encourage cohesiveness by attempting to establish a favorable social climate. Several methods exist for establishing such a climate.

Begin by establishing realistic goals and objectives for the completion of a project. With goals, group members are more likely to feel that they have a specific purpose, a direction for their energies. As the discussion progresses, it may be necessary to modify the goals or to add or subtract some goals from the original list. Such modifications in goal setting are fine and should not be discouraged. For example, some goals can be so ambitious that they are difficult or impossible to reach; modification of such goals can help the group avoid being discouraged. Every group needs a sense of flexibility; rigid observance of rules, regulations, and goals can stifle the problem-solving discussion process. Stated goals also allow the group to judge its progress in relation to the time allotted to the project.

Another way to encourage cohesiveness is for the group to reinforce members' efforts. When one member does good work, other members should recognize the individual efforts and encourage him or her to continue. Such reinforcement also serves to encourage other group members. We all like recognition for our efforts. When we get such recognition, we will be doing our work well to please ourselves and other group members. The result is usually a more cohesive group.

Stressing teamwork—the "we are all in this together" idea—also promotes cohesion. Each member is interested in attaining the group's goals. Members speak of "our group," or "we did it!" The cohesive group is much like a basketball team, on which each team member plays well so the team can win.

Describe, in your own words, three ways of developing a cohesive atmosphere in your group.

(a)

(b)

(c)

- - - - - - - - - - - - - - - - - - -

(a) Reinforce good work completed by group members.
(b) Establish realistic objectives and goals.
(c) Stress teamwork among members.

8.   For a group to be cohesive, the communication channels within the group must remain open. Each member must feel free to express agreement or disagreement with the issues being discussed by the group. Each member should also feel free to talk about the discussion process, to make a statement like "It seems to me we are off the track. We spend too much time discussing irrelevant matters." Members can save the group much frustration and anxiety by indicating problems with the discussion process and suggesting solutions. Comments about the group process, as opposed to task-related questions, are called orientation statements. Many groups withhold comments concerning the process because members fear they may hurt someone's feelings or may seem to be trying to lead the group. Such fears generally serve to repress a potentially serious group problem. Therefore, groups should strive for honesty on the process-related dimension as well as on the task and social dimensions of the group.

(a)   What are orientation statements?

(b)   "There seems to be a conflict over who should be leader; let's decide so we can accomplish group business." Is this an orientation statement? Explain.

- - - - - - - - - - - - - - - - - -

(a)   Comments dealing with the discussion process.
(b)   Yes, because it deals with the discussion process.

9.   Look at the following cases taken from the movie The Poseidon Adventure for signs of cohesion—or lack of it.

Case 1
After the Poseidon capsizes, the Reverend Scott asks Martin to climb up a Christmas tree jerry-rigged to provide an escape route through the bowels of the ship to the rudder area. Survivors of the ship appear passive, lost, and confused. Responding to Martin's pleading, some say, "Leave me alone and go away." One by one the people respond that they are not interested in following Reverend Scott in a gamble for survival. Some issue catcalls, such as "You are all crazy" and "This is where I want to stay." Most just say nothing. Much chagrined, Martin leaves the milling people and exclaims to Scott that the the case is hopeless; the other people will not follow them.

Case 2
Once Reverend Scott and eight others make the gamble and climb up the Christmas tree, the ballroom floods, confirming the correctness of their decision to stick together. Thereafter, they become a team, depending upon one another for survival. Acres becomes an information giver, since he was a ship steward and knows the intricate tunnels and passageways. The group praises him for his tireless efforts, even though he has been severely injured in the initial

capsizing of the ship. Rogo, a police detective, seems to challenge Scott at every turn but risks his own life to rescue Acres from a churning mass of water. Belle, who is obese, is compared to a five-hundred-pound fish by Robin, a small boy in the group of survivors. Robin later apologizes, because he did not mean to hurt Belle's feelings.

At a critical juncture, Scott is pinned under an obstacle, and Belle saves his life in a heroic underwater swim. Rogo, generally abrasive in his interaction with the group, recognizes her efforts with the comment, "You sure had guts, lady."

As each new danger is encountered, all members unselfishly risk their own well-being to see that Robin and his older sister, Susan, are the first to be protected. At one point the group encounters other survivors but gives no thought to following them; rather, they continue to work as a unit in a desperate but firm resolve to follow Scott.

In one poignant scene after Belle has died, Scott says to her grieving husband, "You must go on. Your wife is dead and time is running out." Scott's comments, overheard by Rogo and perceived as cruel, become a catalyst for Rogo to dress Scott down. "Why are you always punishing us? Why is it that you are always the one who says who is to do what and when it will be done?" is the jist of Rogo's attack.

More concerned about completing his mission than defending his actions, Scott ignores Rogo's goadings with a final heroic effort to save the group, which culminates with the loss of his own life. Subsequently, the little band of survivors is rescued, and Rogo affirms Scott's actions as being in the best interest of their group.*

(a) Which case portrays signs of a lack of cohesion? Why?

(b) Which case portrays signs of cohesion? Give some examples.

- - - - - - - - - - - - - - - - -

(a) Case 1. The members appeared passive, apathetic, and quiet, and they had no group identity.
(b) Case 2. This group showed many signs of cohesion. Even though things

---

* These two selections are descriptions of situations from the movie The Poseidon Adventure, courtesy of Twentieth Century-Fox.

appeared hopeless at times, morale tended to be high, and the group worked as a team. Members were praised for good work, arguments prevailed, and disagreement arose from time to time. Members referred to themselves as a group and were willing to make personal sacrifices for the group's welfare. The fact that they stuck together when other survivors were discovered in an interior passageway strongly demonstrated that the group was cohesive. Moreover, Rogo's willingness to challenge the whole decision-making process used by Scott indicated that he felt channels of communication were open to questioning.

SUMMARY

In Chapter 2, we have discussed several interacting factors affecting the small-group discussion process. To isolate such variables out we have focused on the most significant and common factors that interact to affect the problem-solving process in small groups. Of special importance are primary and secondary tension, congruence, cohesiveness, productivity, and commitment. Groups develop over a period of time in a given environment. Understanding these elements affecting the group discussion process can help us to identify and explain why some groups succeed and others fail. The more we understand about these factors, the better we can direct our efforts toward making problem-solving discussions work effectively.

SELF-TEST

The following questions will help you assess how well you understand the material in Chapter 2. Answer the questions and then look at the answers and review instructions that follow.

1. When is primary tension harmful to the small-group discussion process?

2. Which usually takes longer to reach a decision—a cohesive group or a non-cohesive group?

3. Should a group experiencing severe secondary tension be dissolved and replaced by another group?

4. Should a group discourage conflict among members about issues confronting the group?

5.   What effect does congruence concerning social and task issues have upon the group's commitment toward its final decision—positive or negative?

6.   Is it true or false that, according to Carl Rogers, a congruent person is generally perceived as being abrasive or rude?

7.   Which is generally more committed to its final decisions—a cohesive group or a noncohesive group?

8.   Can a group be cohesive on the task level and not on the social level?

Answers to Self-Test

Compare your answers to the questions on the Self-Test with the answers given below. If all your answers are correct, go on to the next chapter. If you had difficulty with any questions, you may want to review the frames indicated in parentheses following the answer. If you missed several questions, you should probably reread the entire chapter carefully.

1.   Primary tension is harmful only if it is allowed to continue and to become the normative or expected behavior of group members. (frames 2-4)
2.   A cohesive group. Members of a cohesive group generally feel free to disagree and often spend much time discussing relevant issues. Noncohesive groups often spend less time in decision making. Such groups are often concerned with expediency rather than with quality decisions. (frames 6-9)
3.   No. It is not necessary to dissolve the group and appoint another. If members of the original group will discuss the issue causing the tension, often the source of the tension can be found and eliminated. Once the tension is resolved, the group can return to productive sessions. (frames 3-4)
4.   Such conflict should not be discouraged. The conflicts should be presented to the group and openly discussed. From such conflict and subsequent discussion may emerge the "best solution" to task problems confronting the group. (frame 3)
5.   Positive. If members honestly express their feelings and reactions to both task and social issues, the group's final decisions will reflect the

input of each group member. Such input is usually essential if the group is to be committed to its final decisions. (frames 5-6, 8-9)

6.   False. Carl Rogers does not suggest a congruent person is perceived as abrasive or rude. (frames 5-6)

7.   A cohesive group. (frames 6-9)

8.   Yes. Cohesion on the task but not the social level is common in groups meeting to discuss topics of concern. (frame 6)

CHAPTER THREE
Approaches to Problem-Solving Discussion

Group problem-solving procedures can follow several patterns, varying in the organization or the blueprint followed for reaching the solution to the problem, depending on the situation. The solution may be found by following a rigid, highly structured procedure or a loose, vaguely defined structure. In Chapter 3 we will examine both a systematic and nonsystematic pattern for problem-solving discussion.

OBJECTIVES

When you have completed Chapter 3, you will be able to:

- Identify and explain a systematic approach to problem solving.

- Identify and explain the five rules for brainstorming.

- Contrast the systematic and nonsystematic approaches, and explain when each approach to problem solving is more desirable.

1. All groups daily encounter problems that can be solved through problem-solving discussion. For the family group the problems may include some of the following: How do we stay within our food budget? When should we trade cars? What do we buy our relatives for Christmas? How can we teach our children not to make fun of others? Many problems in the business world are also ripe for small-group problem solving. For the board of directors of an airline, some problems may be: How can we show a profit when gasoline and maintenance costs continue to rise? Should we sell our mothball fleet of cargo planes? Will the government give us trouble with our advertising? What accounting procedures are appropriate for a new department?

  Such problems may be solved in either a systematic or a nonsystematic manner. The <u>systematic problem solver</u> often defines and limits the problem, analyzes it with a series of questions about its various facets, decides upon possible solutions, selects the best solution, implements it, and reevaluates the solution for possible modification.

The nonsystematic problem solver might ignore the problem, let it escalate until forced to act, go to a friend for advice, or escape from making a decision. Or he or she may think about the problem, take a walk for escape, and then try to solve the problem in a trial-and-error fashion.

Groups, like individuals, may achieve success with either a systematic or nonsystematic method of problem solving. However, we recommend the systematic approach, because it is a rational, planned approach based on a careful study of evidence, which is essential to problem solving. The nonsystematic approach follows no prescribed guidelines. While either approach may lead to the same goal, the systematic approach increases the probability of arriving at the desired goal. Look at the following situation, and answer the the questions that follow:

Case
Paul, a businessman, has a self-concept problem—he is very shy, nonassertive, unhappy, and unnoticed on the job. He seeks help and is placed in a therapy group that meets regularly over a period of time.

At the first group meeting, Paul shares his problem. Group members and the therapist listen empathetically and seek clarification of his problem. His behavior communicates shyness and discomfort.

At the second group meeting, the group and therapist ask Paul to describe how he would like to be. After he completes the description and answers questions, Paul makes a contract with the group to put forth effort to solve his problem with their support.

At the third group meeting, Paul reports that he has to attend a business meeting out of town and feels very uncomfortable about having to meet new people and being in the spotlight when he gives a report. The group members give Paul support and describe how they want him to behave at the meeting.

At the fourth meeting, Paul comes in all smiles. He is full of life, almost gregarious, and reports great progress at the out-of-town business meeting, including a job offer elsewhere.

At the fifth meeting, Paul reports going for a job interview. He feels good and notices overall improvement in his life.

At the sixth meeting, Paul reports he has taken a new job and will be moving away. He thanks the group and the therapist for their help and says goodbye.

What pattern of problem solving does the above series of six meetings illustrate?

_____ (a) systematic

_____ (b) nonsystematic

- - - - - - - - - - - - - - - - - - -

(a) Systematic. A prescribed pattern was followed in solving Paul's problem.

SYSTEMATIC APPROACHES TO PROBLEM SOLVING

2. We will discuss a systematic approach for analysis and resolution of a problem in a group setting. All systematic approaches employ the concept of reflective thinking, which is the process of turning an idea or subject over in your mind in a serious, deliberate, continuous manner. This process suggests a systematic, logical approach to solving a problem. Examine the following conversations, and identify which portrays reflective thinking.

_____ (a) Husband to wife: "You know, at Uncle Ben's funeral today, it occurred to me that we need to give serious consideration to preparing for our own deaths. A number of options have to be reckoned with—flowers versus a memorial fund, burial versus cremation, embalming versus donation of the body to science, church funeral versus a memorial service, to name just a few."
Wife: "Yes, we need to talk about these things. Death is a hush-hush concept that most people ignore until it's too late. I wonder about the merits of purchasing burial lots when we don't know where we might be living, or what we would consider home thirty or forty years from now. And what should we tell our children about our desires for a simple service? Why don't we sit down right now and map out our wishes?"

_____ (b) Husband to wife: "Funerals are scary. I feel so helpless with the bereaved, and the whole scene is freaksville."
Wife: "Makes my skin crawl. Let's talk about death when we're old. By the way, when does the liquor store close? We need to stock up for our hunting trip tomorrow."

- - - - - - - - - - - - - - - - - -

(a) The dialogue concerning planning for death illustrated more reflective thinking.

3. The systematic problem-solving approach uses reflective thinking and is, in fact, called the reflective approach. Based on a book published early in the twentieth century—How We Think, by John Dewey—the reflective approach is a prescription for rational problem solving that carries problems from the felt difficulty to the implementation of a solution.* Careful analysis and logic dictates the solution ultimately applied to solving problems.

Because the reflective approach is widely used, we will consider it in some detail. The reflective approach may be divided into two general phases: the problem-description phase and the problem-solution phase. Within the problem-description phase are two steps, the first of which is definition and limitation of the problem. This step is necessary because members of problem-solving groups must agree at the beginning of the discussion on the meaning of all the terms in the problem or question being raised.

---

*John Dewey, How We Think. Boston: D. C. Heath and Company, 1910.

A group of five surgeons met to discuss the question "What are the pros and cons of transsexual surgery in our society?" Before they could intelligently discuss this issue, the moderator suggested that common meaning should be established regarding the terms in the question under discussion. What terms do you think the group should define to establish commonality of meaning?

– – – – – – – – – – – – – – – – – –

Pros, cons, transsexual surgery, society. For example, by "pros and cons," the group might mean advantages and disadvantages, strengths and weaknesses, favorable and unfavorable implications, or some other dichotomy with subtle shades of meaning. By "transsexual" the group might mean changing the sex from male to female, or vice versa. By "society," the surgeons might mean the community, nation, or some other distinguishable population of people.

4. In addition to defining terms, the group members need to agree upon the boundaries of the problem under discussion, establishing clearly the limitations to be imposed. For example, a group of scientists were discussing the question "What are the implications of current weather phenomena on the future history of mankind?" After agreeing within the group on what was meant by "implications," "current," "weather phenomena," "future history," and "mankind," the scientists found that some limitations needed to be established. Without them the scientists would not know whether they were focusing on weather in a region of a county, an entire country, a hemisphere, the world, or the galaxy. Moreover, they might agree to limit their discussion to certain kinds of weather conditions, such as tornadoes or hurricanes. Or they might limit it to long-term seasonal trends, if the definition of terms has provided the necessary precision. Nevertheless, by raising questions of both definition and limitation we can insure that the group members are on the same wavelength regarding the area of discussion.

Suppose you were a member of a problem-solving discussion group pondering the following question: "What should be the government policy toward socialized medicine?" What possible limitations might be imposed on your discussion?

– – – – – – – – – – – – – – – – – –

A definition of government might serve both to define and limit the discussion to such areas as local, state, or national levels of government. The group also might want to impose limitations of age, income, family structure, and so on, though some of these restrictions might be premature.

5.   The second step of the problem-description phase in the reflective approach is analysis. When we analyze a problem, we separate the whole into component parts. Like a doctor probing to pinpoint the cause of a patient's pain, we must ask what is wrong and what is causing the problem. Many times a group can start this step by using the following questions to make a thorough analysis:

(1)   What is the history of the problem?

(2)   What facts bear on the present situation?

(3)   What are the causes of the problem?

(4)   What are the observable effects of the problem?

(5)   What events or factors produce or bring about those effects?

You may raise other questions, and you may raise some of these but not others. However, the above questions represent the kind of questions important to this analysis step.

Read the following case describing a city council meeting, and answer the question that follows it.

Case
A group of city council members were discussing the problem of potholes in the streets in their town. Maintenance crews were kept so busy repairing the potholes that the crews' energies could not be directed toward the building of much-needed new streets. Mr. Eldenberg, a member of the council and a civil engineer, suggested that the best solution for the problem would be to ban heavy trucks from city streets that were heavily overworked with traffic. Mr. Steele, a concerned private citizen attending the council's open meeting, pointed out that a similar solution had been implemented on Mitchell Street for the two previous years and that the repair needs of Mitchell had not apparantly diminished. Therefore, Mr. Steele suggested that the council explore the possibility that other causes, such as the dramatic variable changes in the weather in recent years, might be contributing to the deterioration of the city streets. Moreover, Mr. Steele asked if other effects had been noticed in the surfaces of the streets besides the obvious potholes.

Which of the two men seemed to be taking a more analytical approach to the problem?

_____   Mr. Eldenberg

_____   Mr. Steele

- - - - - - - - - - - - - - - - - - -

Mr. Steele. With all due respect to Mr. Eldenberg's qualifications, he is solution-oriented before the problem has been properly explored.

6.   Thus the two steps of the problem-description phase of the reflective approach to problem solving are (1) definition and limitation and (2) analysis.

Suppose a group agrees that the term <u>bicycle</u> means "a vehicle with two wheels in tandem, a steering handle, a saddle seat, and pedals by which it is propelled." Which step of the problem-description phase of the reflective approach would the group be applying?

- - - - - - - - - - - - - - - - - -

the definition-and-limitation step

7.   The second phase of the reflective approach is the <u>problem-solution</u> phase. This phase consists of four steps: (1) generation of possible solutions, (2) appraisal of the solutions, (3) selection of the best solution, and (4) implementation.

For the first step, generation of possible solutions, to be most effective, a group must have a wide range of possible solutions to consider. One creative tool which helps nurture ideas is brainstorming.

The strategy of <u>brainstorming</u> is used to generate a quantity of ideas, not to focus on quality. Any decision about which ideas are best is left until the flow of potential solutions has dried up. This increases the group's chances of selecting the best solution. Groups that use the technique usually agree that the greater number of potential solutions, or ideas, the better the resulting solution. The logic behind brainstorming is sound. If the group acted on each potential solution in the order presented, their energies might be consumed in working through many undesirable solutions before the best one was even suggested. Worse, they might adopt a less satisfactory solution simply because it was suggested first.

Responsibility for making the brainstorming strategy operate effectively usually falls to the group's leader. Although the cooperation of the other group members is required, the leader must insure that the flow of potential solutions is uninterrupted throughout the brainstorming session. The reason for focusing this responsibility on the leader is simple: Group members, like most of us, sometimes prefer their own ideas to those of others, possibly because they understand their own ideas better. Thus, people tend to campaign for one idea at the expense of others. But the moment any group member shows a personal interest in one idea or attacks another, the flow of new ideas grinds to a halt. Other group members may also begin to defend pet ideas and, worse yet, some members may withdraw altogether. Therefore, the group leader must support an atmosphere much like that described in the American folk song "Home on the Range," where "seldom is heard a discouraging word." Some groups even report using a police whistle to interrupt group members who cannot resist the temptation to campaign. The choice of technique is up to the group leader, but the challenge remains: to insure that the flow of potential ideas is uninterrupted.

To gain the best results from a brainstorming session, the following five rules should be followed as closely as possible:

(1) <u>Suspend</u> <u>judgment</u>. This rule eliminates criticism of the ideas of other members. Under no circumstances should anyone be allowed

to criticize a suggested solution or to endorse any other solution until
the leader brings the brainstorming session to a colse.

(2) Think wildly. No idea is too strange or too far out to gain a hearing,
since any idea may trigger another member's thinking. Frequently
the combination of one member's suggestion and another member's
modifications contributes to the best solution. This combination is
so effective that it is the subject of the next rule.

(3) Practice piggybacking. Sometimes called hitchhiking on an idea, piggybacking is essentially the process of expanding someone else's suggestion or combining two suggestions. Expansion, combination, and
modification of ideas frequently result in truly creative solutions.

(4) Stress quantity of ideas, not quality. This rule is partially covered
by the first rule, but it is so important that it cannot be overempha-
sized. Only the final decision of the group will determine which suggestion was most acceptable. By then, the quality of those suggestions
which were not chosen will interest only historians.

(5) Make a list. This rule could prove to be the most useful, because
each member needs to know that his or her idea will go into the hopper
with all the other suggestions until a final selection is made. Keep
the list of ideas on a chalkboard or a large illustration pad in front of
the group. Each member can then refer to the list to help spark new
ideas and avoid duplication. The list is also a tangible reminder that
each idea is being treated equally during the actual brainstorming
session.

Brainstorming is characterized by the creativity of its results (the number
of potential solutions to a problem), not by the efficiency with which the results
are achieved. Brainstorming does not work well when the group is under a
deadline; much silence and a healthy measure of completely useless ideas
should be expected. For example, if a sewer-district steering committee is
pressed to solve a municipal sewer problem, the group may be unreceptive to
the suggestion that everyone dig "one-holers" in their back yards; however,
this suggestion is exactly the kind that should be expected in a brainstorming
session. Thus, brainstorming provides a number of challenges to the group
leader. He or she must determine, with the help of other members, whether
enough time is available for use of the brainstorming technique. In some problem-solving situations—for example, the judging of the Miss America pageant—
the means of solution are established, and brainstorming would only cause confusion. The group leader who thoroughly understands brainstorming will recognize when the situation and the group are appropriate for the technique.

The following case will illustrate brainstorming as a problem-solving technique and show the leader's responsibility in managing its use. Read the study
thoroughly.

Case

When the residents of a growing resort area created a new school district, an
almost infinite number of new problems arose to be solved. One of the less

immediate tasks was the selection of a mascot to represent the new high school. Although the grandstands for the new football field were almost complete, the coach was able to order only basic protective equipment, because the school had no colors, no school song, and no name for the football team. When the superintendent of the new school district invited the coach for dinner in early June, you can imagine which problem dominated the conversation. The coach counseled against involving the new football players in the project, so the superintendent decided to call the leaders of some school-affiliated groups to determine which group would work on the problem. The next day the superintendent approached the president of the new PTA, who said her group would gladly take volunteers for a mascot committee from its ranks at the July meeting. The superintendent suggested that valuable time would be lost in waiting for a mascot committee to be formed, but the PTA president declined to act without a vote of the membership. The chairman of the new school board, a local banker, was delighted to get a call and told the superintendent he had been thinking about that very problem. He offered to discuss the matter with his advertising manager and to phone back in the afternoon. He also promised that he would handle any questions about the choice that might arise at the next school board meeting. The superintendent said he was just shopping for ideas and promised to keep the banker's offer in mind. When the superintendent finally located the president of the parent's booster club, he discovered that the group's only interest was in selling season tickets. The booster club members did ask, however, to be kept informed so that they could place an early order for windbreakers with the appropriate colors and insignia.

Then the superintendent noticed the school's new cheerleaders practicing at the edge of the football field. He asked Jo Anne, the head cheerleader, what name they were building their cheers around. The cheerleaders complained loudly that they were stuck on that point. Jo Anne explained that they were also having problems in ordering their uniforms. When the superintendent asked if the girls would tackle the problem of selecting a mascot, they quickly agreed.

Kathy, who had been head cheerleader at her former high school, suggested that the group use her soundproof family room for their first work session on the problem, and the cheerleaders agreed. By the time the small talk had died down the next evening, it was 7:30, and Kathy's father had promised to chase everyone home at 10:00. They easily agreed that the problem was to select a mascot which could be used as a theme for the athletic teams, on the masthead of the school newspaper, and in the yearbook, as well as in cheers and the school song. They agreed that their aim at this first session was to get as many ideas as possible. The cheerleaders had all been thinking about the problem since talking with the superintendent, and their ideas began to flow easily. Jo Anne soon realized that it would be impossible to keep track of more than a few suggestions at a time, and she asked Kathy for something with which to make a list. Kathy volunteered one of her father's large illustration pads and a felt-tip marking pen.

When the illustration pad had been set up, Kathy asked for each cheerleader's suggestions and began writing them down. Jo Anne suggested "Rams,"

Kathy said "Lions," Bill proposed "Stallions" or "Trojans," and Nancy mentioned "Sharks." While Kathy was writing Nancy's suggestion, Mary Lou said, "There's not an ocean within 500 miles of here. Let's try 'Indians.'" Pat, who had arrived late, said he was working on the school song and that "Indians" would fit in well. He and Mary Lou began to talk about the lyrics, and finally Jo Anne had to interrupt. Jo Anne explained to Pat that before he had arrived, the group had agreed to spend the first meeting only on ideas and that discussion of the ideas would begin at the next meeting. Pat said he understood and that "Trojans" worked into the lyrics, too. Then, as Pat finished talking, he looked at the list and said, "That's it! 'Trojans' and 'Stallions,' like Trojan horses. Let's try 'Trojan Horses.'" Mary Lou added, "How about 'Lions Sharks!'" and the others all laughed. Emmy suggested "Bombers." As Kathy was writing it down, Bill said "Dive Bombers," Mary Lou added "Rockets," and Jo Anne said "Screamers."

Thirty minutes later the room was quiet. Kathy slumped beside an illustration pad literally covered with names. Bill said "Barracudas," but Jo Anne suggested they call it a night before Kathy could even write it down. Bill didn't complain. Emmy noted that it was only 9:00, but the others were too tired to respond. As they filed out of the house, Kathy's father asked if everything had gone well, and Mary Lou said, "Zebras, Ticks, and Mushrooms," which ended the discussion.

Now let's test your understanding of brainstorming with the questions from the above case.

(a) If the superintendent and the coach had felt the mascot problem required a speedy decision rather than a creative one, who would have been given the job?

(b) Could the superintendent determine by talking to the different group leaders which group would be best suited to solving the problem? Why?

(c) Why did the superintendent bypass the PTA?

(d) When Jo Anne explained to Pat the cheerleaders' aggreement to work only on ideas the first night, what was she trying to do?

(e) When Pat looked at the list and said, "That's it! 'Trojans' and 'Stallions,' like 'Trojan Horses,'" what was he doing?

(f) Which rule was Kathy following throughout the brainstorming session?

(g) When Mary Lou said, "There's not an ocean within five hundred miles of here," which rule was she breaking?

(h) When Emmy suggested "Bombers" and Bill followed with "Dive Bombers," Mary Lou with "Rockets," and Jo Anne with "Screamers," what rule were they following?

(i) Mary Lou's suggestion of "Lions Sharks" would be an example of what?

(j) By completely filling the illustration pad, would you say the cheerleaders had followed rule 4?

(k) When Jo Anne explained the brainstorming rules to Pat, what kind of atmosphere was she trying to create?

- - - - - - - - - - - - - - - - - - - -

(a) The banker; (b) Yes, because the group leader is responsible for setting the scene for brainstorming; (c) The PTA would have waited so long there would not have been enough time for a creative solution; (d) She was trying to make sure the flow of potential solutions was not interrupted; (e) Piggybacking, or hitchhiking his ideas; (f) Rule 5—make a list; (g) Rule 1—suspend judgment; (h) Rule 3—practice piggy-backing; (i) Rule 2—think wildly; (j) Yes, they stressed quantity; (k) An atmosphere where "seldom is heard a discouraging word."

8. Brainstorming is a tool for gathering the greatest quantity of potential solutions to a single problem. If a group cannot afford the time necessary for brainstorming solutions, we suggest that at least two essential questions be raised in the selection-of-possible-solutions step in systematic problem solving:

(1) What are the possible solutions to the problem?

(2) What is the exact nature (kind, order or general character) of each solution as it is originally conceived?

Let's examine how this process might work.

Case

Suppose three business partners leased a trailer court to another party with the understanding that either party (lessors or lessees) could cancel the agreement by giving a ninety-day written notice. After advancing the first year's payment of $1,000, the lessees became disgruntled and gave notice of cancellation after three and a half months of the agreement had transpired. No part of the original agreement had been violated. Nevertheless, the lessee requested the return of the entire year's advanced rental fee. The owners planned to analyze the problem together. However, because time was a critical variable, they decided to ask one partner to draft letters before their meeting, each offering a different solution to the problem. That partner drafted five letters which, in essence, proposed the following:

(1) The request for payment return was denied.

(2) The request for payment return was honored.

(3) The request for payment return was answered with a compromise suggestion of partial return of funds.

(4)   The request for payment return was to be turned over to an attorney for analysis and legal advice.

(5)   The request for payment return was to be brought before a mutually agreeable nonpartisan committee and its decision honored.

Are these all possible solutions to the problem? _____

- - - - - - - - - - - - - - - - - -

yes

9.   Do the solutions seem to merit further consideration and evaluation?

- - - - - - - - - - - - - - - - - -

Solutions (1), (2), (3), and (5) address the assignment given the partner. Solution (4), while having merit, sidetracks the original request. However, it might be left as an item for discussion by the business partners, since the later appraisal step is where weaknesses and strengths of solutions would be carefully considered.

10. After identifying possible solutions, the next step in problem solving is to appraise each solution. Appraisal of solutions should generally start with the establishment of the criteria any acceptable solution should fulfill. Discussion of criteria before this stage is not recommended, because it can inhibit the generation of creative ideas. The following questions often prove helpful in appraisal:

(1)   How does each solution relate to the criteria established?

(2)   What will be the consequences of adopting each solution?

(3)   To what extent will each solution answer the question or solve the problem?

(4)   What are the relative merits and demerits of each solution?

(5)   What are the advantages and disadvantages of each solution?

The questions will vary, depending upon the nature of the problem or question under deliberation. As before, you may skip some and add others. But these questions represent a good starting point for appraising solutions in the reflective problem-solving approach. Notice that the appraisal questions involve relating each solution to established criteria; this process can help the group identify what basic requirements are essential for a solution to be acceptable.

For example, the parks and recreation department of a small city decided to discuss the topic "What can be done to facilitate bicycle safety in our parks and nature trails?" The body of decision makers had completed its third meeting, having defined and limited the problem, analyzed the problem, and brainstormed possible solutions. It then met to appraise the possible solutions that had been generated. The group began its discussion by establishing the criteria any solution must meet in order to be included for further deliberation. Without reviewing the twenty solutions that had been suggested at the previous meeting, the group agreed that any solution must (1) accommodate the needs of pedestrians as well as cyclists; (2) require no additional floating of bonds by the city; (3) minimize the need for additional police protection after dusk; and (4) maintian the present bicycle pathways without major alterations in their basic structure. In essence, these criteria became a "filtering device" through which all solutions had to pass to be considered. Moreover, this criteria–building mechanism provided a safeguard of objectivity for the appraisal of solutions.

Objectivity reinforces the analysis of strengths and weaknesses of possible solutions. Often a group member feels special allegiance or emotional involvement with certian solutions, and his or her jugment may be distorted. Agreeing upon criteria can help overcome these attachments or at least justify the inclusion or elimination of certian solutions from consideration. Brainstorming can also be used to generate criteria for analysis of solutions. Let's look at an example.

Case

The board of directors of a large photography firm established the following list of criteria for the hiring of a new sales manager for the corporate headquarters:

(1) experience in personnel management

(2) five years of sales experience

(3) ability to be a self-starter

(4) human relations training

(5) degree in liberal arts

(6) field experience in selling the corporate product

(7) favorable image

(8) strength of character

(9) creative ideas

(10) knowledge of competitive lines

(11) communication skills

(12) ability to organize meetings

(13) technical familiarity with photographic processing.

The chairman of the board of directors composed a letter integrating what she felt were the most essential criteria and mailed the letter to the prospects referred to the board. Examine the following letter, and identify the essential criteria she gleaned from the list of criteria.

James Perch
7140 East 52nd Street
Lawrence, OK 46226

Dear Mr. Perch:

The purpose of this letter is to inform you that Interstate Studios of Indianapolis, Indiana, is seeking a sales manager effective June 13, 1980. Yours is among the names given to our board as one who may be qualified to fulfill our needs. Therefore, we are writing to inquire if you are interested in being considered for this position.

For your information we have included some information about our company and the city of Indianapolis. Please find enclosed a brochure about our fine city.

We are a family-owned business devoted to the sale of photographic services through educational institutions. Our enterprise began in a modest fashion in 1930 and has grown to a company with a sales force of one hundred men and women in a fifteen-state area. Besides our sales representation we have a photographic production staff of forty men and women. Our present sales manager, Mr. Bob Kruger, will be retiring in July.

The minimal requirements we have established for our new sales manager include having field experience in photographic sales and services. Since we are excited about the potential marketing of new products and services, we would like someone with innovative ideas, communication skills, and experience in personnel management. While we would like someone with a liberal arts background, we would not exclude a graduate in business administration at the undergraduate level. We are in a position to offer a salary commensurate with educational preparation, ability, and experience.

Please feel free to call or write us about this position. A specific job description is available upon request. We look foward to hearing from you in the near future.

Sincerely,

Paula Burke
Chairman of the Board
Interstate Studios, Inc.

As reflected in this letter, what criteria did the board appraise as most important?

- - - - - - - - - - - - - - - - - - - -

field experience in photographic sales and services, innovative ideas, communication skills, experience in personnel management, and a liberal arts undergraduate background

11. By establishing in advance the values the group felt should be manifested in a sales manager, the board of directors was able to avoid any special interests or emotional involvement by certain members of the group which might distort judgments and lessen the quality of the overall decision-making process. Establishing criteria before they appraised particular applicants increased the board's objectivity.

After criteria are agreed upon, the appraisal phase can be strengthened by raising and responding to other appropriate questions, such as those on page 55 (frame 10). Review that list of additional questions now. Then read the following case, keeping in mind the appraisal questions you feel are relevent to the situation.

Case

A personnel manager, in the process of hiring a PBX switchboard operator, has narrowed the applicants down to four and must choose one of the four for the position. The manager invites you and three other unit supervisors to assist in the final selection process. As a group you agree that you desire an efficient, reliable, experienced operator who would plan to stay with the organization for a long time. Your group reviews the following data about each applicant:

(a) Bertha Jackson is forty-four years old. She is a black woman who has worked for twenty-six years as a cleaning woman in a local office building. Since her job is at night, she has taken a course during the day and learned to operate a PBX board. Bertha wants this job because it pays more and is easier on her physically. She has a son in college and two children in high school. Her husband deserted her ten years ago. Her references indicate that she is a hard worker and gets along well with others. The personnel manager has two concerns: (1) Her voice isn't particularly pleasant, and (2) she has no actual experience in this work.

(b) Phil Jones is twenty-one years old and is a student in his junior year at the local university. Phil is from a poor family and has to work his way through college. For two years he was a PBX operator in his dorm, but when the campus went to a different system, PBX operators were eliminated. While the personnel manager likes Phil's experience, he is concerned that he might not be accepted too well in an all-female office.

Also, Phil was once charged with making an obscene phone call to the women's dorm. Charges were dropped when the woman he called failed to pick out his voice when listening to a series of recorded voices.

(c) Ann Marie Johnson is thirty-four years old. She has been a housewife for ten years. She has two children, and her husband is a successful executive. Money is not a problem. However, Ann feels that her life is boring and unrewarding. The children are in school, and she feels the need to get out and do something. She worked as a PBX operator for three years before she was married and enjoyed that kind of work very much. Tests indicate that she is very bright and could do a fine job.

(d) Carol Chaplin is a beautiful woman. Twenty-one years old, Carol has an exceptionally pleasant, outgoing personality. The personnel manager noted that, in tests, her voice was by far the easiest to listen to. Of the candidates, she is the most proficient on the switchboard. Carol comes from a wealthy family. Her father has provided her with a nice apartment and a new car. In her hometown she has worked as a receptionist and PBX operator. References praise her as an exceptionally capable and likeable girl. While she seems to have everything necessary for this job, the manager is concerned that Carol thinks of herself as a free spirit. He is afraid that she won't stay long in any one place. Nevertheless, she has excellent qualifications.

As a group, your task is to decide which person should get the job. In addition, you must provide the personnel manager with specific reasons for your decision. Record the questions you think should be asked to facilitate the appraisal process:

(a)

(b)

(c)

(d)

(e)

- - - - - - - - - - - - - - - - - - -

Some possible questions are listed; you may have thought of others:
(a) What are the criteria we have established for applicants?
(b) How does each applicant measure up to these criteria?
(c) What will be the probable consequences of hiring each applicant?
(d) To what extent will the hiring of each applicant solve the need for a PBX operator?
(e) What are the advantages and disadvantages of hiring each applicant?

12. Once solutions have been appraised, the group reaches the third step in problem solving—group members must agree upon the solution they think is best. Occasionally a group is unable to reach consensus (general agreement)

concerning which solution is best. On such occasions the group may find it necessary to resort to the democratic process of voting. However, voting is seldom necessary if group members agree upon criteria, maintain a spirit of objectivity, and raise and honestly answer the appropriate appraisal questions.

Let's go back to our PBX case to see if we can reach consensus. Which applicant would you hire?

_____ (a) Bertha Jackson

_____ (b) Phil Jones

_____ (c) Ann Marie Johnson

_____ (d) Carol Chaplin

Why would you hire the applicant you checked?

- - - - - - - - - - - - - - - - - - - -

(c) We would hire Ann Marie Johnson because she appears to be efficient and reliable and has the experience desired by the group. Additionally, we feel that she will best meet the longevity requirement and does not have the potential liabilities of the other candidates. Our concern would be her level of motivation and, in a formal interview, we would want to focus on why her life is boring.

13. The last step in the problem-solving phase of the reflective approach is implementation. The "test of fire" for any solution is to put it into practice. One must put the solution to the test and observe the results. Naturally reappraisal and modification may be necessary with even the best solutions.

Once a solution is implemented, the problem may not be solved. The group must monitor the success of the solution and evaluate and modify it as necessary, as the following case shows.

Case

The building-and-grounds committee of the local Jaycees was asked to hire a custodian to handle the cleaning of the Jaycees' new building. The president of the organization also asked the committee to establish a standard set of procedures for the custodian to follow in meeting weekly, monthly, and yearly cleaning responsibilities. Moreover, the committee was to establish a fee structure for paying the custodian they hired.

The committee mapped out what they felt was a complete list of weekly, monthly, and annual cleaning needs of the building. Furthermore, to test the list, each committee member took a turn at the weekly cleaning of the building, religiously following the outlined guide for cleaning. In due time, the committee hired a custodian and paid him $10 per week—a rate they determined was fair based upon the average time of two hours it took each member of the committee to clean the building.

Proud of their work, the building-and-grounds committee reported to the president of the Jaycees that the building care was in good hands. Much to the committee's dismay, their custodian quit after just one month. The committee promptly met with the disgruntled custodian to listen to his reasons for quitting. They learned that the building had been made available to the Boy Scouts, the Lions Club, and numerous other organizations. No provisions for cleanup had been made by the organizations using the building. Therefore, the newly hired custodian had had to clean up the building several times per week. Upon hearing the custodian's plight, the committee recommended that the following policy be adopted as a modification to their original proposal for custodial fee structure: "When the building is made available to nonmembers for special events, a fee shall be established, and a substantial portion of that fee will go to the custodian for services rendered." Additionally, the committee decided to schedule a monthly meeting with the custodian for airing any problems he might be having in the care of the building.

Now that we've completed our survey of this systematic method of problem solving, let's review the whole approach. See if you can fill in the missing steps of the reflective approach outlined below.

(a) Problem-description phase

    (1)

    (2)

    Problem-solution phase

    (1)

    (2)

    (3)

    (4)

(b) Which of the above steps were the building and grounds committee applying when they modified their custodial fee structure?

- - - - - - - - - - - - - - - - - -

(a) Problem-descriptive phase
    (1) Definition and limitation of problem
    (2) Analysis of problem

    Problem-solution phase
    (1) Generation of possible solutions
    (2) Appraisal of possible solutions
    (3) Selection of the best solution
    (4) Implementation of the solution

(b) The implementation step, which includes evaluation and modification of the solution.

(Note: Two other systematic approaches to problem solving have been gaining attention only recently: the single question method and the ideal question method. However, because these methods are so new, we have chosen not to discuss them in this book, until time and experience have better demonstrated their usefulness.)

NONSYSTEMATIC PROBLEM SOLVING

14. The nonsystematic approach in problem-solving discussion is sometimes called the free approach. As the term suggests, the group does not attempt overtly to order discussion along the lines of the systematic approaches we have covered. Nonsystematic problem solving follows no preconceived pattern; rather, discussion simply evolves freely from what group members consider important to the problem situation. Thus the approach relies heavily upon group members' ability to contribute effectively to advancing the problem-solving process. In essence, members of the group considering a problem must recognize opportunities for clarifying issues and bringing to light their honest opinions on a topic. The aim of the free discussion is to bring out the group members' various perspectives on the problem situation.

Groups that adopt a free approach to problem solving generally feel that we should stop insisting upon a highly perscriptive, mechanical approach to problem solving and that we should instead seek true freedom, a relaxed atmosphere, free communication, and an atmosphere not dictated by structure. With a nonsystematic approach, they argue, members can be more productive because the climate is permissive. While there may be some merit in these arguments, a group without a plan too often makes a quick decision but not a high-quality decision. Nonetheless, in some situations, a nonsystematic approach can have real merit, at least for a time. Let's examine some settings where a nonsystematic approach may be most effective.

A nonsystematic approach is most useful when the objective facts of a case are not contested and where issues are highly charged emotionally and bring out conflicting attitudes and feelings. Such questions are least likely to be resolved through the imposed structure of systematic problem-solving approaches. In fact, whenever open conflict based on strongly held feelings and attitudes results, systematic problem solving should be suspended and a free discussion employed. Attempts to impose structure at such points typically result in resentment, more unproductive disruption, or withdrawal of some members from further contribution to the problem-solving discussion.

However, given the volatile nature of issues usually involved, a nonsystematic approach requires an active leader to facilitate equitable communication. Such a leader must insure that minority opinions are freely expressed without fear of reprisal from either the majority or the leader. Therefore, in free discussion the leadership function is active but strictly limited to maximizing each member's input. The leader may contribute knowledge and experience, but he or she must do so without imposing a personally held

preference for a particular outcome from the discussion. In short, a nonsystematic approach may work best when secondary tension resulting from severe
interpersonal conflicts occurs. Look at the following example to see how a
nonsystematic problem-solving approach might apply.

Case

A city council of a small midwest city had been involved in several discussion
sessions in which it was determined that the city would have to comply with a
new state law regulating the collection and disposal of solid waste. The council agreed that private haulers in the city were not in compliance with methods
of collection and disposal now required by state law. In prior sessions the
council had defined the problem and analyzed its ramifications. Possible solutions to the problem had been suggested, and at this session the council was
actively engaged in determining the relevant criteria any probable solution
should meet.

At this meeting three council members became involved in a hotly contested dispute with another council member. The three council members had
tendered a solution to bring the aspects of solid-waste collection and disposal
under the city's control to assure compliance with the new state regulations.
They recommended letting bids for an exclusive contract by the city with a
private collection-and-disposal firm. The opposing council member contended
that this solution might put other local firms out of business, so that such a
solution to the problem was "anti-democratic" and "threatened the principles
of the free enterprise system." This member was adamantly opposed to his
colleagues' solution and refused to consider other possible solutions until the
issues regarding this one were resolved.

The mayor, acting as the problem-solving discussion leader, had set the
agenda for this meeting during the prior week. He had not forseen open conflict over any contested solution. However, the mayor astutely recognized
that these council members were now expressing deeply felt attitudes and feelings rather than discussing objective facts. He also saw that with the three-
to-one odds against the one member, and the council's strict adherence to a
systematic agenda, that member was becoming resentful and had begun to
withdraw from further involvement in productive discussion.

How would you attempt to resolve this conflict, if you were mayor?

- - - - - - - - - - - - - - - - - -

To nurture the support of all members, we recommend suspending the systematic agenda and employing a nonsystematic approach until the conflict is resolved.
Remember that free discussion is most valuable for conflict resolution in

situations where attitudes and feelings strongly conflict and where objective facts are not contested. As leader in this free discussion, the mayor should actively facilitate communication, provide information, and insure minority rights or expression until the conflict is resolved and a systematic approach is again appropriate.

SUMMARY

In Chapter 3, we have contrasted systematic and nonsystematic approaches to dealing with problems. We identified and explained a systematic approach to problem solving—the reflective approach. This approach includes six steps: in the problem-description phase, (1) definition and limitation of the problem and (2) analysis of the problem; and in the problem-solution phase, (3) generation of possible solutions, (4) appraisal of possible solutions, (5) selection of the best solution, and (6) implementation of the solution. We also discussed brainstorming as a creative process for generating ideas. Finally we explored some situations in which a nonsystematic approach to problem solving might have merit. Administrative staffs, organizations of all kinds, committees, and other formal or informal groups should find these approaches useful in their efforts to improve the decision-making process.

SELF-TEST

The following questions will help you assess how well you understand the material in Chapter 3. Answer the questions and then look at the correct answers and review instructions that follow.

1. Compare and contrast the systematic and nonsystematic approaches to problem solving.

2. What is the role of brainstorming in group problem solving?

3. Several brainstorming rules were identified and explained. Which is most important? Why?

4. The systematic approach to problem solving has two phases. Identify the two phases, and the steps within each phase.

5. When might a nonstructured approach to problem solving have merit? Why?

Answers to Self-Test

Compare your answers to the questions on the Self-Test with the answers given below. If all your answers are correct, go on to the next chapter. If you had difficulty with any questions, review the frames indicated in parentheses following the answer. If you missed several questions, you should probably reread the entire chapter carefully.

1. A systematic approach to problem solving is a rational, carefully planned approach to solving a problem; it is common sense put into action. Systematic problem solving is designed to bring about a high level of rationality by charting a carefully planned course of action and then following it.

    A nonsystematic approach, in contrast, follows no predetermined course of action. The hallmark of this approach is freedom, a lack of structure, and extreme flexibility.

    Both the systematic and nonsystematic approaches are acceptable means for solving a problem; the nonsystematic may take the "scenic route," while the systematic stays on the main highway. (frame 1)

2. Brainstorming can be a very effective technique for stimulating the gener-
    ation of ideas essential for solving problems. Results of groups using
    brainstorming suggest that group members produce more ideas than they
    would have other wise. Since idea generation is vital in solving problems,
    brainstorming is an important tool for groups to understand and use. The
    more ideas that are available, the greater probability of having worthwhile
    ones from which to choose. (frames 7-9)

3. We discussed five important rules for success in using brainstorming
    methods: (1) suspend judgment; (2) think wildly; (3) practice piggybacking;
    (4) stress quantity of ideas; and (5) make a list. While all five are very
    important, and keeping a list may be the most useful because of its obvious
    practical benefits, suspending judgment is probably ultimately most impor-
    tant. The quickest way to kill enthusiasm and dampen the production of
    ideas is to start criticizing them. (frames 7-9)

4. The systematic approach focuses on two phases: problem description and
    problem solution. The problem-description phase has two steps: (1) defi-
    nition and limitation of the problem and (2) analysis of the problem. The
    problem-solution phase has four steps: (1) generation of possible solutions,
    (2) appraisal of possible solutions, (3) selection of the best solution, and
    (4) implementation of the solution. (frames 2-13)

5. When strong feelings are expressed and secondary tension is apparent, it
    is better to forget about structure and to permit full and free discussion
    so all can vent their feelings.

    Once interpersonal conflicts are brought out in the open and dealt with
    under a judicious leader, the group is often able to return to a more struc-
    tured approach for careful deliberation of the substantive issues before the
    group. (frame 14)

CHAPTER FOUR
Preparation for Problem-Solving Discussion

Chapter 4 will focus on how to prepare for effective discussion by collecting relevant information. We will explore the many sources of information available and the best ways to obtain and evaluate it.

OBJECTIVES

When you complete this chapter, you will be able to:

- Distinguish between personal knowledge and research data.

- Recognize when preparation is needed.

- Identify and apply various methods for collecting information.

- Use library organization and research aids that enhance data collection.

- Develop a basic plan for conducting interviews as a method for data collection.

- Take careful notes while collecting information.

- Analyze and evaluate information collected for use in problem-solving discussion.

1. Discussion groups are often criticized for "pooling ignorance." Conventional wisdom may describe a camel as a horse designed by committee. Sometimes committees and problem-solving groups do pool ignorance and fail to arrive at meaningful solutions, but this need not be the case. To solve a problem through a decision-making process, a group depends upon the ability of its members to discuss intelligently, which requires preparation. Preparation means that each member must have sufficient information and knowledge about the topic for intelligent decision making. Preparation for a group discussion is a responsibility shared by all group members. The amount of preparation

needed will depend upon what the group already knows and the nature of the problem. As we shall see, preparation for discussion involves <u>introspection</u>, <u>data collection</u> (or <u>research</u>), and <u>evaluation</u>.

Preparation for discussion can be viewed from both an individual and group perspective. In Chapter 3, we noted various elements of the reflective problem-solving approach, including defining and limiting the problem and analyzing the problem. These essential group tasks require an information or data base. Where will this information come from? Some will come from the members' own knowledge and experience, but many problems, due to their importance or complexity, require additional information—research.

So far, we have emphasized the importance of the group—group interaction, group sharing, and group problem solving. While the collective efforts of the group are important, preparation involves much individual effort and commitment. Group members begin preparation for a problem-solving discussion at different points, depending on the mode of group formation (also called group emergence). In the following examples, observe the different methods of group formation, and note when the group members begin preparation.

Case 1
Ed See, a member of the Theater Department, received notice that he had been appointed to a university-wide committee charged with the task of evaluating the master's degree program in the Business Department. The notice also stated that the evaluation committee chairman would contact Professor See within three weeks to schedule the first group meeting. A week later, See received a large package containing course schedules, course offerings, student enrollment figures, faculty assignments, and other "raw" data related to the master's program in business. See realized that this committee assignment would require more than a few quick meetings and a rubber-stamp approval.

See began reading and organizing the information he had received, but he soon realized that he didn't have enough information to form a complete picture of the business program. In order to better prepare for the committee meeting, See decided upon a threefold course of action: First, he would survey the university's catalog of course offerings and compare the business program with other master's degree programs; second, he would interview two of his friends who taught in the business department and ask for their opinions concerning the strengths and weaknesses of the business program; and, third, he would go to the library and look through business journals and magazines for articles discussing what the business world considers important for students in master's programs.

Case 2
Ben, Laura, Kris, Nina, and Sam were all enrolled in a course called Small Group Communication. For the final class project they had been randomly assigned to one of four task groups. Each group was to identify a campus-wide problem, study the problem, and then, during the last week of the term, present a panel discussion. The main objective of the panel discussion would be to propose a solution for the problem. After class the five task-group members were drinking soft drinks and coffee in the Student Center and discussing the assignment.

After fifteen minutes of moaning and groaning about Professor Winsor, the assignment, and all the other classwork they had to complete, Kris remarked, "Look, this isn't getting us anywhere."

Ben replied, "I know one problem that no one does anything about and that's crossing Highway 13 from the men's dorms to the main campus."

"I never thought of it that way," said Sam, "but you're right. I was almost hit by a car this morning."

"Laura expressed an alternate point of view. "You guys think you've got it bad. I'm a commuter, and every morning I have to sit in my car and wait for you guys to cross over from the dorm. Some mornings I just feel like laying on the horn and plowing right through all those jaywalkers."

"Hold it," said Nina. "We've found our problem. Dorm residents can't get across the street, traffic is held up, and we women who use the East Athletic Field have trouble crossing the highway."

The group members continued giving opinions and sharing experiences until they realized that, before they could solve the problem, they needed concrete, specific information. Ideas for solving the problem (crossing guards, over/under passes, and the like) were only abstractions. They had to explore cost factors, find out how many pedestrians used the crossing, and identify who was responsible for the crossing—the university, the city, or the state. As a group, they composed a list of research questions including:

(1) How many cars travel through, and how many pedestrians cross the highway during the day?

(2) What is the frequency of accidents in the crosswalk?

(3) What alternative traffic patterns or structures have been used in other communities to solve similar problems?

(4) What are the typical costs involved in redesigning the crossing?

(5) Who has the responsibility for change—university, city, or state?

(6) Are federal funds or grants available for this type of project?

Having transferred the gaps in their knowledge into research questions, the group members divided the questions among them. Each group member promised to find answers for his or her questions and then report back to the rest of the group.

(a) Describe how the groups were formed in each case.

   Case 1

   Case 2

(b) Each group in Cases 1 and 2 had a problem to solve. How did the groups differ in the selection of the problem?

(c) Preparation for the two discussion groups began at different points. Describe when preparation began for each group.

Case 1 group

Case 2 group

- - - - - - - - - - - - - - - - - -

(a) In Case 1, Professor See was appointed to his group; in Case 2, the students were randomly assigned to a group.

(b) Professor See's group (Case 1) had its problem assigned to it, while the students in Case 2 selected a problem of mutual interest.

(c) Ed See (Case 1) began his preparation <u>before</u> the first meeting (we don't know about the rest of his group); the students in Case 2 began their preparation <u>after</u>.

2. In the two cases in frame 1, both Ed See and the students realized the need for additional preparation. Ed See evaluated his own personal knowledge and the information sent to him by the committee chairman and found that he needed to do additional preparation. See did this before the first group meeting; it would be nice if all group members arrived at the first meeting prepared to discuss the problem. However, as shown by Case 2, group members often do not clearly recognize the problem that confronts them, nor do they know the extent of the knowledge held by other group members until the group meets. Once the group has met, members have the responsibility, individually or collectively, to prepare for future meetings. Research in small-group communication shows that one of the leading causes of failure in problem-solving groups is lack of member preparation.

In frame 1 we described preparation as involving three steps: introspection, data collection or research, and evaluation. At which of these three steps are Professor See and the students?

- - - - - - - - - - - - - - - - - -

Introspection. They are assessing what they know before proceeding.

3. While you can refer to many sources of information, the first place to look is at yourself. Each individual brings to the group a unique set of <u>experiences</u> and knowledge—this fact is one of the strengths of the group process. Suppose that you are a sales manager, and your company's sales are declining. As a member of the management team, you are to meet with other company officials to discuss the problem: declining sales. How might you <u>prepare</u> for this problem-solving discussion?

- - - - - - - - - - - - - - - - -

Introspection, with special attention to your knowledge and experiences. Perhaps the decline is seasonal, or perhaps the sales force is understaffed. In any event, note what you already know before charging off to explore other sources of information.

4. In the process of assessing personal knowledge, be careful not to confuse personal opinion with facts. Facts are concrete; that is, facts exist apart from our inferences and beliefs, while opinions derive from our inferences and beliefs. Read the following example, and see if you can determine which statements are based upon fact and which are drawn from opinion.

Case
Jacky's, a women's clothing retailer, operated several stores in a Mid-western city (population above 75,000). The firm purchased a similar store in a small college town located in the same state. A large inventory of spring and summer fashions, including a large proportion of stylish sundresses, were shipped to the new college-town branch to mark the reopening of the store under Jacky's management. The inventory failed to attract customers, and sales failed to offset expenses. The local manager reported the following:

(a) Sales are 60 percent below the rate of the city branches.

(b) The women in this town don't appreciate fine ladies' wear.

(c) Our prices tend to be higher than the prices of the previous management.

(d) College coeds, the largest consumers of women's clothing in this area, dress informally and have less need for the type of stock we carry.

(e) The school is a suitcase college; all the students go home on weekends to spend their money.

Review the five statements reported by the store manager, and indicate whether they are based on fact or opinion.

(a) Fact_____ Opinion_____

(b) Fact_____ Opinion_____

(c) Fact_____ Opinion_____

(d) Fact_____ Opinion_____

(e) Fact_____ Opinion_____

- - - - - - - - - - - - - - - - -

(a) Fact. A store manager would have these data.
(b) Opinion. In this case a subjective value judgment has been drawn.
(c) Fact. A store manager should know how his or her prices compare with the prices of others.
(d) Fact. While this statement may seem to indicate an inference on the part of the manager, a clothing store manager would be expected to know, with

some degree of certainty, the dress habits of his or her customers.

(e) Opinion. Without careful study, any comment about the spending habits of potential customers remains an opinion. Also, the use of the term "suitcase college" indicates a subjective value judgment.

5. In addition to distinguishing between fact and personal opinion, you must also assess the reliability of your knowledge of the subject or problem. For example, history books tell us that World War II began during September 1939, when German forces attacked Poland. However, Germany did not declare war on Great Britain and France; rather Great Britain and France declared war on Germany—a "fact" which still leads some Germans to believe that England started the war. Evaluate the reliability of your personal knowledge by reviewing the basis for that knowledge.

For information based upon education: Was the learning experience adequate in scope, time, resources, and instruction?

For information based upon work experience: Was the work experience adequate in length of service and type of work performed? Was the climate or environment typical or atypical of the work experience?

For information based upon personal observation: Were you in an adequate position to observe the event fully? Were you physically able to observe (to see, hear, touch, and so on) the event? Was your observation clouded by inferences and beliefs?

If a thoughtful review of your personal knowledge raises questions of reliability, then additional preparation is needed.

The extent to which a group can rely on the personal knowledge and experience of the group members depends on the nature of both the group and the problem. For example, the Downtown Chamber of Commerce should have within its membership business and professional people who could plan promotional activities which are designed to attract shoppers to the downtown business district. On the other hand, this same Chamber of Commerce may need to do additional preparation, including research, to qualify for the Federal Model Cities Program. In the first case, sales promotion is associated with the group's normal activity; the membership is comprised of merchants, business people, and professionals who already have skills and knowledge suited for the task.

The second case, Model Cities, would seem to require additional preparation. Federal programs are often mired in red tape and regulations; applications for federal monies often entail extensive studies, surveys, and environmental-impact statements. These cannot just be developed at a breakfast meeting without preparation.

When the topic or problem confronting a group requires more than personal knowledge, the discussion participants will need to conduct a serious research or data collection.

A group of college students, appointed by the Student Government Association, desire information on what types of facilities should be included in a

new student activity center.   Should the students rely on personal knowledge
or on research?   Explain.

- - - - - - - - - - - - - - - - - - -

Research.   The students may have many good ideas, but they would probably
lack both the experience and the knowledge to decide, without additional study
and research, which types of facilities are practical or economically possible.

6.   Once we decide that additional data would enhance our preparation for discussion, we should consider alternate places for research.   The word "library"
might bring to mind a quiet place to read a newspaper, find that long-sought
mystery, or locate a do-it-yourself stereo guide, but a library is much more.
A library is not only a storehouse of knowledge, information, and data; it also
provides reference services to those who seek help.
       Libraries are often divided into several sections to make finding informa-
tion easier.   Even small libraries have reference sections, periodical sections
(magazines and newspapers), and a general section.   College and university
libraries as well as large city libraries are often further subdivided into subject matter sections: music library, science library, technology library, hu-
manities library, and so on.   Reference sections, sometimes called the reference library, contain materials used as general references:

Encyclopedias	Book summaries
Indexes	Plot outlines
Catalogues	Maps and charts
Bibliographies	Telephone directories
Dictionaries	Statistical abstracts
Biographical abstracts	Yearbooks
Record books	Who's Who directories

The holdings of any reference section vary from library to library, and the
above list indicates only part of what may be discovered in a reference library.
In addition, a library staff member is usually assigned to the reference area
for the single purpose of helping people find research material.

       If you know little about library organization, what should you do when re-
searching in a library?

- - - - - - - - - - - - - - - - - - -

Ask a librarian.

7.   Assume that you are interested in learning more about public health care
in the United States.   You have been told that national health-care organizations
will send information upon written request.   Where in the library would you be

most likely to find a listing of such organizations?

- - - - - - - - - - - - - - - - - -

In the reference section. An Encyclopedia of Organizations does exist.

8. The president of your local chapter of the League of Women Voters has phoned and asked you to prepare biographical sketches on the district congressional representatives and the two United States senators from your state. The league meets tomorrow night. What section of the library would be most useful to you and what materials might you look for?

- - - - - - - - - - - - - - - - - -

The reference section. While you could check to see if books had been written by or on your congressional representatives and senators, your research time is short, and they may not have been in office long enough to warrant books having been written about them. Your best bet is to check in one of the Who's Who series (which include national, regional, and subject area books), or in biographical encyclopedias and abstracts.

9. In most libraries, the index of books, authors, and subject matter is called the card catalogue. The major holdings of the library will be listed in this index. Similarly, magazine articles are indexed by specific titles, authors, and subject areas in the Reader's Guide to Periodical Literature. Special fields of study, such as education, psychology, or business, have their own special indexes—ask for them. While the Reader's Guide provides an index to popular, mass-circulation periodicals, these special indexes will direct you to professional and scholarly periodicals, such as Harvard Business Review, Personnel Psychology, Education, Social Work, Administrative Science Quarterly, Abnormal Psychology, Quarterly Journal of Speech, or Journalism Quarterly.

What is the first place you should look for a book on pollution control?

- - - - - - - - - - - - - - - - - -

the card catalogue

10. If you wanted to compare how Newsweek, Time, and U.S. News and World Report reported the Democratic National Convention held at Chicago in 1968, what should you consult?

- - - - - - - - - - - - - - - - - -

the Reader's Guide to Periodical Literature

11. Articles written on T-Group training methods are often found in the Journal of Applied Behavioral Science. Without looking at every issue of this periodical, what type of library index would help you locate such articles?

_____ (a) The Reader's Guide

_____ (b) The card catalogue

_____ (c) A special index

- - - - - - - - - - - - - - - - - -

(c) A special index. In this case, the Education Index would be most helpful.

12. Several years ago, Elaine Morgan published a controversial book titled The Descent of Woman. Which library index could quickly tell you if your library had a copy of the book? Describe how you would use the index.

- - - - - - - - - - - - - - - - - -

The card catalogue. Since the card catalogue is an index of titles, authors, and subjects, you could look for the author's name in the index, or you could look for the book's title. If you were unsure of the exact title or the author's name, you could then look through the subject section of the card catalogue under the heading "women."

13. Suppose that your library does not have a copy of The Descent of Woman, but you still wish to read the book. Where in the library might you find the book's publisher so that you might write for a copy?

- - - - - - - - - - - - - - - - - -

In the reference section. Most reference libraries have a publication called Books in Print which would provide the needed information. Many libraries can also arrange for you to borrow the book from another library; ask your librarian if interlibrary loans are available to you.

14. Community and college libraries are not the only sources of information. Do not overlook private professional libraries. Many professionals—such as the clergy, doctors, lawyers, teachers, and people in business—maintain personal libraries related to their vocations. The use of private, professional libraries may require special arrangements or conditions, but if other sources of information are unavailable, then a private collection may be your only option. Local, state, and national government agencies, departments, and officials will provide information upon request. The United States Government Printing Office, for example, is an especially good source of information.

Name two alternate sources of research materials other than public libraries.

- - - - - - - - - - - - - - - - - -

professionals and the government

15. Occasionally, the information a group needs in preparing for a discussion is not contained in books, magazines, or other printed matter—it's contained in people. In this case, the group member, or the entire group, should consider interviewing as a method of data collection. Interviewing can be a rewarding and valuable method of data collection, or it can be a complete waste of time and energy—depending upon how discussion participants approach interviewing.

A full presentation of interviewing techniques is not within the scope of this book, but several suggestions and guidelines are presented as an aid. First, interviewing should not be viewed as a shortcut to research—a means of avoiding library research. A well-planned and well-conducted interview takes as much effort as reviewing back issues of Business Week. Second, avoid interviewing just for the sake of interviewing. Third, plan your interview strategies in advance. As you plan your interview strategies, consider the following points:

(1) Decide what kinds of information are needed; then select for interviewing those persons who can best provide the information.

(2) Develop a list of questions (an interview schedule) in advance of the actual interview. Word the questions clearly, avoiding loaded biased questions.

(3) Determine how you will record the answers to your questions—note taking, tape recording, or memory. Remember, some people do not like to be tape-recorded. Ask permission if you plan to use a tape recorder.

(4) Make an appointment for the interview. Don't just drop in for a chat!

(5) Arrive on time for the interview.

(6) As you begin the interview, review your reason for conducting the interview. Don't fire questions immediately.

After you have completed the interview, review the information obtained. If circumstances required that you rely on your memory, immediately put the information in writing. If you took notes, check for legibility and gaps due to personal shorthand methods. If you were able to tape-record the interview, a written transcript containing the most vital answers could be made and copies distributed to the other group members.

Case
Bob arrived five minutes late for his interview with the county welfare director. He made no apology for his tardiness, but he did joke about the state of

traffic and parking, while he glanced around the director's office for an outlet where he might plug in his tape recorder. The director remarked that it was against office policies to tape-record interviews. Bob made some cute remarks concerning "Big Brother" listening and then asked for a sheet of paper on which to take notes. As he was handed a sheet of paper, Bob asked the director, "What do you think of this welfare mess?"

The interview described above began poorly and got worse. Bob committed several errors in preparing for and conducting his interview with the welfare director. Describe the errors you observed in Bob's interview.

- - - - - - - - - - - - - - - - - - -

First, Bob arrived late for the interview. Sometimes lateness cannot be avoided, but an apology would seem necessary. Second, Bob did not secure permission to tape the interview; he had to be told not to do so. Third, he gave the impression that he was not prepared; he lacked paper. Fourth, his first question was poorly stated and inappropriate. Fifth, Bob seemed to lack good common sense. His jokes and cute remarks were in poor taste.

16. After four straight levy and bond election defeats, the local school board formed a citizens' advisory committee to aid the passage of future levy and bond proposals. In addition, the citizens' committee would serve as an independent group to examine the building, equipment, curriculum, and staff needs of the school district and report to the public. While the subcommittees on building and equipment could observe and tour the various elementary and secondary school buildings within the district and then make recommendations, the curriculum subcommittee faced highly subjective questions: What is the status of the curriculum? What improvements need to be made? How can curriculum improvements be implemented? What future curricular needs should be planned for?

Ms. Muller, a member of the curriculum subcommittee, felt that information to answer some of these questions could be obtained by interviewing the dean of the School of Education at a nearby state university. The dean was both a recognized authority in curriculum planning and a former school-district superintendant in a large metropolitan school system.

If you were Ms. Muller, how would you proceed in preparing for and initiating the interview with the dean?

- - - - - - - - - - - - - - - - -

Compare your procedure with Ms. Muller's. First, the curriculum subcommittee examined and discussed the curriculum then offered by the school district. Through this discussion the committee raised questions concerning the curriculum which Ms. Muller incorporated into a list of interview questions. Second, Ms. Muller carefully reviewed the curriculum guide provided by the school district so that she could ask additional questions if the interview provided the opportunity. Third, she decided to take notes rather than tape-record the interview; she felt more opinions might be obtained if the dean believed that he wouldn't be quoted verbatim. Fourth, she phoned the dean's office, explained her purpose, and made an appointment for the following week.

17. At the close of the interview, Ms. Muller thanked the dean for the interview. She then proceeded to her car for the trip home, but before leaving she looked through the notes of the just-completed interview. Why did she return to her notes?

- - - - - - - - - - - - - - - - -

Initially, she would check for legibility and gaps in her notes. Additionally, she could write down other information which she had committed to memory during the interview.

18. Once information sources have been located, whether through library research or interviews, the information must be carefully recorded or copied. There are three important reasons for careful note taking: (1) reliability, (2) accountability, and (3) ethics. Unless the original materials can be brought to the discussion meeting, a participant must rely on notes. Inadequate or sloppy notes are not reliable and may lead to poor decision making due to poor information. During the course of the discussion, a group member may be asked to quote specific data or access the accuracy of the statement—in this case, the participant becomes accountable for his or her statements. The author or source of the cited material spent time and energy in the preparation of the book, article, or report cited—that person deserves credit or acknowledgment. To claim another's work as your own is not ethical.

If you are transferring information from the original to notes (five-by-seven-inch notecards are easy to work with, but some people prefer to use notebooks), begin by placing the author(s) name(s) at the upper left-hand corner of the card. If no author is cited, indicate the absence with the notation "no author given." Follow the author's name with the title. If you are citing

an article from a newspaper, journal, magazine, or the like, include the title
of the publication. Below the author's name and title, indicate the city of publication, the publisher or sponsoring organization, the date of publication, and
the page or pages from which the information is cited. Materials edited from
other sources should include the name of the editor.

David B. Sutton and N. Paul Harmon. Ecology: Selected
Concepts. New York: John Wiley & Sons. 1973, p. 17.

"A concrete example of a cybernetic system is a heater-
thermostat system whose set point is the point (temperature)
at which the householder sets the dial."

Following your bibliographical entries, begin the actual note taking. Carefully transfer the material to your cards. Be sure to place quotation marks
around data directly quoted. If you paraphrase or summarize information,
indicate, in the margin, that you are paraphrasing or summarizing.

David B. Sutton and N. Paul Harmon. Ecology: Selected
Concepts. New York: John Wiley & Sons. 1973, p. 17.

Paraphrased

A common example of a cybernetic system is the home
furnace using a thermostat. The "set point" of this system
is the temperature setting of the thermostat.

It is also helpful to follow a similar procedure with interview notes. Place
the name of the individual interviewed at the upper left-hand corner of the note
card. After the person's name, indicate the time, date, and location of the interview. Beneath this information, state the qualification of the person interviewed—plant supervisor, county judge, social worker, college professor,
bank officer, eyewitness, or the like.

Fred Clark. 2:00 p.m. September 12, 1977. His office.
County Welfare Director

Question: How will changes in the Federal Food Stamp
          Program affect the college student population
          living in this community?

Answer: College students will need to prove need for assis-
        tance before receiving aid. This will include a re-
        view of the students' parents' resources.

In frame 1 of this chapter, we described a group of college students who
selected a discussion problem concerning a highway pedestrian crossing.
Let's rejoin the students at their second meeting. At this point, we find them
discussing the information collected since the last group meeting. (You may
wish to return to frame 1 and reread the account of their first meeting before
proceeding.)

Case
After several minutes of random exchanges, the group settled down to begin
concentrating on their discussion problem. Kris presented a summary of traffic accidents occurring in or near the crosswalk which she had compiled from
newspaper accounts.

"Where did you find those newspaper stories?" Laura asked.

Kris described how the local newspaper maintained a "morgue" of past
issues which, upon request, was open to researchers.

"Good work," said Ben. "But what years do those accident reports co-
ver?"

Kris checked her notes and replied that her summary covered all the issues from September 1973 to May 1977—the four years since the campus enrollment had begun to increase.

Following Kris's summary, Sam reported to the group the results of his
interview with the city public works director. "Mr. Wells, the public works
director, told me that on an average day 1,150 cars travel through the crosswalk."

Before Sam could continue, Nina cut him off with, "Sam, your information
doesn't stack up with mine. I found a report at the library which stated that
during peak hours no more than one hundred cars per hour pass through the
crosswalk, while the rest of the day fewer than fifty cars intersect the crossing."

Ben, sensing a possible conflict, asked Nina, "Which hours of the day
were described as peak hours? If we knew the hours, perhaps the figure you
gave will add up to a total close to Sam's information."

"I wish I could tell you," replied Nina, "but I didn't write it down."

Ben volunteered to go to the library and recheck the traffic report. "Nina," asked Ben, "what was the name of this report?"

"I believe that it was called Annual Report of Traffic Flow, or maybe it was called An Analysis of Traffic Flow and Street Usage. You'll find it."

In the above case, the students who presented information used three different sources of information?

(a) Where did Kris find her summary of traffic accidents?

(b) Where did Sam get his information?

(c) Where did Nina locate her traffic report?

- - - - - - - - - - - - - - - - - -

(a) in the morgue of the local newspaper
(b) through an interview
(c) in the library

19. While newspaper articles, personal interviews, and library research provide equally good sources of information, notice the striking difference between Kris's report and Nina's. Compare Kris's and Nina's reporting of their research. (Remember the three important reasons for careful note taking discussed in frame 18.)

- - - - - - - - - - - - - - - - - -

Kris seems to have done a much better job of note taking than did Nina. Nina's information didn't give the impression of being reliable nor was she accountable for the accuracy of her information. Nina's note taking was poor, and information poorly recorded does not aid the group's decision-making process. In addition, Nina's failure to record properly the correct title (presumably the author's name was also omitted) presents a question of ethics. While Nina may not have overtly laid claim to another's work, her failure to properly identify the report makes use of another's work without giving proper credit.

20. Once members of a discussion group have conducted their research and carefully recorded their information, they should analyze and evaluate the information. Critical thinking is an essential feature of group decision making. Critical thinking involves testing our information to determine whether it is relevant, accurate, and the best available. Too often we accept written

information and the testimony of others just because the information is in print or because the sources claim to be authoritative. We should also apply critical thinking to testing our ideas and solutions as we attempt to solve problems.

Relevant information is information that directly relates to the topic. For example, the rising cost of food continues to be a serious concern for most American consumers. The high cost of fresh meat has been singled out as an especially vivid example of how inflation affects the buying power of our dollars. During public discussions concerning food prices, an official of the Agriculture Department stated that Americans had little cause for complaint and that meat prices are significantly higher in foreign countries—in parts of the Soviet Union, quality meats were not available at any price. While Americans may fare better at the meat market than their Russian counterparts, is the Russian example relevant to the topic under consideration? We think not. In large part, the Russian agricultural and economic system cannot be compared to the American system; while the Russian example may have a psychological soothing effect, it is not relevant to solving the problem.

During a student discussion of the topic of women's rights, one member quoted an opponent of the Equal Rights Amendment who claimed that the ERA would mean common public restrooms. After a brisk discussion of the advantages and disadvantages of common public restrooms, one member of the group observed that the restroom example was irrelevant to the question selected for discussion—equal political rights for women.

Irrelevant information may or may not be bad information. Discussion groups often spend large amounts of time discussing interesting but nonetheless irrelevant research data. As your group analyzes and evaluates its information, routinely apply the question of relevance—does the information directly relate to the discussion topic?

Case
After receiving a 600-dollar gas and electric bill, the church council of Bethlehem Church met in special session to discuss ways to conserve energy and thus lower the utility bill. Larry (a), the council president, opened the meeting by reviewing the church's utility bills for the last five years. His review included statistics which indicated that the recent gas and electric bill was three times higher than any previous bill during the five-year period. Bill (b), an elder, remarked that inflation and the Arabs were a fact of life, and we might as well get used to paying higher utility bills. Marilyn (c), one of the trustees, agreed, but she wasn't ready to give up. "This building is over twenty years old, and I believe that we can do many things to save energy." Jim (d), a member of the finance committee, felt that the church should reduce the number of activities and services during the cold months and thus reduce costs through reduced use of the building. Needless to say Roger, the pastor, vetoed that idea. Joe (e), another of the trustees, said that the attic space above the main auditorium lacked insulation—insulation would lower the costs by 20 to 40 percent. Glen (f) agreed and suggested that new weather stripping be installed around all doors. "I think we should refuse to sell grain to the oil sheiks," remarked Herbert (g). "Then they'd bring the price of oil down."

Most of the above statements about the plight of Bethlehem Church contained information which could aid the church council in finding a solution to the utility bill problem. However, some of the statements were not relevant to the specific problem. Evaluate the statements made by each council member as either relevant or irrelevant.

(a) Larry's review of past utility bills _____

(b) Bill's statement on inflation _____

(c) Marilyn's belief that the building could be improved so as to save energy

_____

(d) Jim's statement that services should be reduced _____

(e) Joe's idea concerning insulation _____

(f) Glen's idea of using weather stripping _____

(g) Herbert's grain-withholding idea _____

- - - - - - - - - - - - - - - - - - - -

(a) Relevant. A review of past events would aid in making decisions.
(b) Irrelevant. Discussion of inflation, while an important issue, would side-track the group.
(c) Relevant. Improvements are a logical course of action.
(d) Relevant. Reducing services, while distasteful, would be worth discussing.
(e) Relevant. Insulation is obviously helpful to the situation.
(f) Relevant. Weather stripping is helpful, as is insulation.
(g) Irrelevant. A grain boycott wouldn't solve the church's immediate problem.

21. In addition to the relevance of information, several other tests and assumptions should be kept in mind as you and your group evaluate source material. The following case is adapted from a newspaper article with the headline "Nobel Winner Says Blacks Have Lower IQs."

Case
Dr. Alfred Thompson stated today that, as a group, Blacks display lower IQs than the white population. Thompson also stated that further federal expenditures on poverty programs and special-education projects will not raise IQs among inner-city Blacks.

Dr. Thompson earned his Ph.D. at the University of Chicago in 1948. He was awarded the Nobel Prize in Physics for his work with high-temperature fusion of nonmetallic conductors. Dr. Thompson is an advisor to the NASA Deep-Space Probe Project and currently heads the Physics Research Department at Wilson Research Institute.

Thompson's remarks were made at a reception following a conference on national goals. During the conference, several Black speakers questioned the government policy of spending large sums of money on space research.

The American Psychological Association and The National Education Association objected to Dr. Thompson's remarks.

When evaluating the <u>accuracy</u> <u>of</u> <u>information</u> used in a discussion, consider whether the source cited is an expert in the subject area. In the above case, Thompson is a recognized expert in what field? _____

- - - - - - - - - - - - - - - - - -

physics

22. The study of intelligence, the improvement of IQ levels, and the testing of IQ would seem to be related to psychology, education, medicine, or sociology. From what we know about Thompson from the case in frame 21, can he be considered an expert in these areas?

- - - - - - - - - - - - - - - - -

No. From his background, he expresses only lay opinion.

23. In the Thompson case in frame 21, we might be mislead into believing that Blacks have lower IQs due to a phenomenon known as authority transfer. Authority transfer involves a person's real credibility, reputation, or knowledge being associated with a subject or issue for which they are not a recognized expert. For example, physicians in America enjoy high levels of public trust and confidence, and often we observe a physician's credibility projected into nonmedical activities. Titles such as "doctor" and "professor" along with academic degrees (Ph.D., M.D., D.D.S., J.D., and others) should not be interpreted as meaning "expert" on all subjects. Always evaluate the credentials—that is, the training, experience, reputation—of individuals cited as expert sources. Also, be alert to signs that indicate bias or vested interest; experts may testify in such a way that their own interests benefit. An agricultural expert may testify that grain supports be increased; that same expert may own a wheat farm.

In the Thompson example, what title might mislead newspaper readers through authority transfer?

- - - - - - - - - - - - - - - - - -

Nobel winner; also Ph.D. and NASA affiliation. In essence, Thompson's credibility earned through accomplishments in physics may be transferred to a subject for which he lacks adequate credentials.

24. If the average newspaper reader pays attention to only the headline and first paragraph, he or she might miss a section of the newspaper article which

casts doubt on Thompson's motives. What information, in the case in frame 21, signals a possible conflict of interest?

- - - - - - - - - - - - - - - - - -

Several Black speakers questioned government spending on space projects, which implied that money should be spent on social programs—health, education, housing, welfare, and others. The space program and NASA are specially related to Thompson's interests, which might induce him to belittle critics of space exploration.

25. The accuracy of sources of information may depend less on training and experience than on the physical and psychological ability of the source or witness to observe properly the incident or condition described. If a discussion group must render a decision based upon the testimony of sources which describe an event or condition, then those sources should be evaluated along the following guidelines:

(1) Physical ability. Does the source possess adequate vision, hearing, taste, and so on, to allow accurate description?

(2) Position. Was the source in a position or location which enables accurate description?

(3) Ability to perceive. Was the source's emotional state such that the source could report accurately? Was the source sober and/or not under the influence of medicine or drugs which would cloud perception? And does the source possess adequate emotional and maturity levels to enable proper description?

An eyewitness describes in perfect detail the events of a crime. The witness saw the incident from a third-story window at 10:30 p.m. The scene of the crime was measured at two hundred feet from the window casement. The street has but one overhead light located at the opposite end of the block.

Would you accept the testimony of the witness just presented in the example above? Explain why or why not.

- - - - - - - - - - - - - - - - -

The testimony of this witness should be doubted; in evaluating the accuracy of this witness we should check the ability of the witness to see the event. The vision of the witness should be checked—especially night vision. Also, we might wish to determine the position of the witness relative to the line of sight to the incident: standing directly at the window, standing back in the room and looking out the window, or standing in the room attending some activity (watching television, cleaning, or the like) and glancing out the window. It makes a difference.

26. A Hollywood film, Twelve Angry Men, provides a good example of a group evaluating the accuracy of information. In this film, a jury of twelve men must decide the guilt or innocence of a young man charged with the murder of his father. On the surface the case seemed to be rather cut and dried; the "facts" of the case pointed to guilt. However, several members of the jury encouraged the group to evaluate the testimony of the two eyewitnesses—the foundation of the prosecution's case. Below is a summary of the jury's evaluation of the testimony of one of the eyewitnesses—an elderly man who lived in the apartment just below the scene of the crime.

> The old man said that he was lying in his bed when he heard the boy and his father arguing in the room directly above his bedroom. When he heard the sound of a body falling on the floor, he rose from his bed, walked to his door, opened the door just in time to see the boy racing down the stairs.
> Can we believe the testimony of the old man? One member of the jury remembered that the old man seemed to drag one leg; another recalled that the old man admitted having had a stroke the year before. The distance from the witness's bed to the door of his apartment was forty feet. The route from the bed involved crossing the bedroom, turning into the hall, traveling down the hall to the door, unlocking the door, and then looking out to the steps. The old man stated in open court that it took him fifteen seconds to travel from his bed to the front door. The time at which he heard the body fall coincided with the testimony of the second witness who looked out from her apartment directly across the street from the murder scene. In between the apartment of the second witness and the apartment where the crime occurred was an elevated subway track. The second witness saw the crime through the unlighted passenger cars of the train as the train traveled past both apartments. The old man also heard the train, which linked the testimony of both eyewitnesses.*

The jury attempted to recreate the old man's journey from his bed to the door, but before we look at the jury's evaluation of the old man's testimony, how would you rate the testimony?

---

*This selection is a description of a situation from the television play Twelve Angry Men by Reginald Rose.   Copyright ⓒ 1956 by Reginald Rose.

- - - - - - - - - - - - - - - - -

The majority of the jury members doubted the testimony of the old man. First, in their attempt to reconstruct the journey from the bed to the door the best that they could do was forty-five seconds—not fifteen. Considering the old man man's physical condition, he could not have reached the door in time to see clearly who was coming down the stairs. Second, elevated subways make a great amount of noise; the old man claimed that he heard the body fall as the train passed. It seemed unlikely that the old man could hear a body fall with severe background noise produced by the train. Third, the witness also testified that he heard the boy and the father arguing earlier in the evening. Perhaps he confused the earlier argument with the argument leading to the crime. The boy testified that he had argued with his father earlier in the evening but had left the apartment. A member of the jury, himself an old man, stated that perhaps the witness, desiring a moment of attention and fame, made his perception consistent with his desires and not reality.

27. While a particular piece of evidence may seem to be relevant and reasonably accurate, remember that one example or one quotation or one eyewitness account may not be the best data available. Other, equally good and sometimes contradictory information may go undiscovered from a lack of either individual or group preparation. As your group evaluates its information, ask whether the data is the best available. Have we searched far enough? Have we accounted for both personal and editorial bias which may influence our sources? Have we ignored other points of view? For example, the authors have observed several student discussions of the John Kennedy assassination controversy, and no group drew their evidence from sources other than a few sensationalized paperback books. Not a single student discussion member had ever read either part or all of the Warren Report in spite of the fact that it was available in our college library. The Warren Report may be in error, but does a group have enough information from which to make a decision without having read the report?

Suppose that you heard a television interview of former California governor Ronald Reagan in which he stated his opposition to the Panama Canal Treaty. Mr. Reagan is a noted American conservative. Would you conclude that conservatives oppose the treaty?

- - - - - - - - - - - - - - - - -

It would be wise to look for additional information. For instance, Senator Barry Goldwater, a prominent conservative politician, and William F. Buckley, a well-known conservative writer and speaker, support the treaty, as did John Wayne, who was often associated with traditional and conservative causes.

28. Picture yourself enrolled in a college sociology sourse. As a class requirement, you are assigned to a group which must study and report upon the effects of pornography on society. Suppose that your roommate is a regular subscriber to Playboy magazine and that a recent issue of Playboy contains an article which states that Denmark, which has very liberal attitudes concerning pornography, has experienced a reduction in the rate of sex-related crimes. The conclusions of the article imply that unrestricted pornography leads to a reduction in sex-related crimes.

     Would you feel confident in using the Playboy article as the basis for your preparation for the group discussion?

- - - - - - - - - - - - - - - - -

No. It would be unwise to rely upon only one article or one piece of information, especially with regard to a topic like pornography, about which opinions vary widely.

29. There is a second reason for not relying entirely upon one source of information. As you evaluate source material, remember that all publications have, to some degree, a built-in editorial bias. Editorial bias may be positive or negative, depending upon the nature of the publication and the subject presented. It is simply a fact of life that publications reflect the philosophies and politics of their owners and readers. Editorial bias does not necessarily imply false or distorted information. It might mean that all sides of an issue are not reported on an equal basis or that certain facts or characteristics are emphasized while others are ignored. Unless you know the editorial policy or bias of a publication, you may sometimes find it difficult to discern whether the information is reflecting a bias or the actual events. One way to detect possible bias is to compare how similar publications treat the same subject. If, for instance, Playboy, the National Catholic Reporter, Time, and Newsweek all expressed similar views on a proposed drug-enforcement act, you could be reasonably sure that the reports by any one of these publications is fairly accurate.

     Other than the problem of having only one source, do you see a potential editorial bias inherent in the Playboy article? Explain.

- - - - - - - - - - - - - - - - - - - -

Yes. Playboy's coverage of positive results stemming from liberal pornography laws may well reflect an editorial bias. Playboy is considered porno-
graphic in some communities, and its manner of reporting pornography may
be a defensive tactic. (Note: The Playboy example is hypothetical.)

SUMMARY

Chapter 4 focused upon the need for preparation in problem-solving discussion.
Preparation for discussion is both a group and individual responsibility involving the collection of relevant information, with the amount of preparation depending upon the nature of the problem and what the group already knows about
the problem. The process of group and individual preparation for discussion
involves introspection, data collection or research, and evaluation.

Group members should inspect and review what they already know, both
collectively and individually, about a given problem and determine the relative
strengths and weaknesses of their knowledge. If they decide that additional
data are needed, they should consider alternate sources of information. Libraries, public and private, are important storehouses of information; government offices and agencies also are useful sources of information. When the
type of information needed by a discussion group is not available in printed
or document form, the group should consider conducting interviews of people
who have special knowledge or experience. Once the group has collected the
necessary information for discussion, the group should evaluate whether it is
relevant and accurate and whether it is the best available information. Preparation means that each group member has sufficient information and knowledge about the topic or problem to make intelligent decisions.

SELF-TEST

The following questions will help you assess how well you understand the material in Chapter 4. Answer the questions, and then look at the answers and
review instructions that follow.

1. Problem-solving discussion groups are often criticized for "pooling ignorance." What can we as group members do to avoid pooling ignorance?

2. A certain amount of the information a person uses in a discussion comes

from the member's own _____ and _____

_____ .

3.   Preparation for discussion involves what three elements?

4.   What guidelines would you use to evaluate your own personal knowledge of a problem or subject which will be discussed by your group?

5.   What determines whether a group can rely on its collective personal knowledge and experience to solve a problem or whether the group must conduct additional research to solve a problem?

6.   Libraries are often divided into several sections to make the finding of information easier. What section would be the best place to start most research?

7.   Explain what the card catalogue, Reader's Guide to Periodical Literature, and special indexes like the Education Index are, and describe the types of materials these library aids would enable you to find.

8.   What should you consider as you plan your interview strategies?

   (a)

   (b)

   (c)

   (d)

   (e)

   (f)

9.   Why is careful note taking important?

10. When we apply critical thinking to the information collected in group problem solving, what do we do?

11. When evaluating the accuracy of information obtained from an "expert," we should keep in mind two basic criteria. What are they?

    (a)

    (b)

12. What factors would you consider when evaluating the testimony of an observer of an incident?

13. Suppose a neutral third party reviewed the research findings of your group and asked, "Are these the best data available?" What would that party be asking?

14. Whenever we collect data from printed sources, we may encounter the problem of editorial bias. What is editorial bias, and how can we deal with it?

Answers to Self-Test

Compare your answers to the questions on the Self-Test with the answers given below. If all your answers are correct, go on to the next chapter. If you had difficulty with any questions, you may want to review the frames indicated in parentheses following the answer. If you missed several questions, you should probably reread the entire chapter carefully.

1. Prepare to discuss. (frames 1-3)

2. knowledge and experience (frames 1-5)

3. introspection, data collection (research), and evaluation (frames 1-5)

4. Review the basis of your knowledge. If what you know is from an educational experience, was that experience adequate? If from a work experience, was that work experience adequate for you to make a judgment? If from the basis of observation, were you physically and mentally able to observe adequately? (frames 5-6)

5. the nature of the group (and its experience) and the nature of the problem (frame 5)

6. the reference section (frames 6-8)

7. All are designated to help researchers locate information more easily. The card catalogue is a general index of the library's holdings, cross-indexed by author, title, and subject matter. It is the best aid in locating books contained in the library. The Reader's Guide to Periodical Literature is an index to articles published in popular periodicals such as Time, Popular Science, Newsweek, Ladies' Home Journal. It is also cross-indexed by author, title, and subject matter. The Education Index is one of many special indexes designed to help one find information in professional and academic periodicals. The Education Index is also cross-indexed by subject, author, and title. (frames 6-13)

8. (a) Decide what information is needed.
    (b) Develop a list of interview questions.
    (c) Determine recording method.
    (d) Prearrange the interview.
    (e) Arrive on time.
    (f) Plan an opening for the interview—don't just fire questions.
    (frames 15-17)

9. You should have reliable information, you are accountable for your information, and as a matter of ethics you should give credit for another's work. (frames 18-19)

10. Test our information to determine if the data are relevant, accurate, and the best available. (frames 20-29)

11. (a) Is the person a true expert in the subject area?
    (b) Does the person have a vested interest which might cause us to doubt his or her motives? (frames 21-24)

12. Consider the observer's physical ability to see or hear the incident. Consider whether the observer was in a position to observe the incident. Consider whether the observer was in an emotional or mental state that would result in a proper description. (frames 25-26)

13. The third party would be asking if the group had searched far enough or examined a wide variety of source material, if it had ignored other points of view, and if it had accounted for possible personal or editorial bias in its research materials. (frames 27-29)

14. Editorial bias is a built in bias found in nearly all publications. It involves the philosophy or politics or social reflection of the publisher and/or readership of a particular publication. We can deal with editorial bias by seeking information from a variety of information sources. (frame 29)

CHAPTER FIVE
Roles in Problem-Solving Discussion

Chapter 5 is concerned with the roles group members assume as they interact in the group process. First, we will discuss the various roles, and then we will explore cases illustrating them.

OBJECTIVES

When you have completed this chapter, you will be able to:

- Identify and describe the eight characteristics of effective group leadership.

- Identify and describe group task roles, group building and maintenance roles, and self-centered roles.

- Explain why the group task roles and the group building roles are usually required for effective group productivity.

- Explain why the self-centered roles are destructive to the group process.

1. As we interact with other people, we each assume various roles—patterns of behavior that depend upon the environment and the people with whom we are interacting. For example, with our parents, we assume the role of a son or daughter; with our teachers, we assume the role of a student; and with our employers, we assume the role of an employee. Our roles depend upon the requirements of the situation and the other people involved. In various roles, we respond differently. We interact differently with our parents than with our lovers, for example.

For all of us to take on roles is perfectly healthy and natural. However, if we are dishonest in portraying these roles, we experience difficulty. We may find ourselves fabricating stories in order to maintain the false images we have projected. For example, some people, in the role of student, like to project the image of being quite secure, when actually they are not. They refuse to demonstrate any anxiety about classes or other academic matters; they do not want their peers to realize that they, too, have weaknesses and sometimes need help. In projecting secure images when they are really anxious and frustrated, such people are not being honest in the student role. Dishonest portrayal of roles can lead to much frustration and often to interpersonal conflicts with our associates. The solution is simple: Be honest as you live your various roles.

Group members can also be dishonest in the roles they project. For example, a male member may project himself as the "big man"—the one who talks all the time, the one who constantly jokes, the one who demands to practice leadership. This person may be trying to gain attention when he would really be more comfortable—and more productive—being a follower in the group. If he is allowed to play the "big shot" role, both he and the group suffer. Roles can enhance or obstruct the problem-solving process, as we shall see. When entering a group, offer the group the person you are, not the person you think you should be. As a result, you will be a happier, more productive member, and the group will greatly benefit from your contributions.

Mark had just returned from his sociology class where roles had been the topic of discussion. As Mark thought about the class, he realized that he played a variety of roles, including those of son, student, lover, employee, and friend. Mark also realized that his behavior was different within each of his designated roles. He certainly did not act the same with his girlfriend as with his employer.

(a) In your own words, define roles.

(b) Mark portrays several roles. Does this variety of roles present him any problem?

- - - - - - - - - - - - - - - - - - -

(a) Roles are patterns of behaviors we assume based upon the environment and the people with whom we interact.
(b) We all assume a variety of roles. This variety of roles presents no problem as long as we are honest as we assume the various roles.

3. Once we assume a particular role with people, they expect us to remain fairly constant in portraying that role. For instance, if you always play the clown at parties, people will begin to expect such behavior from you. Should you then decide to remain quiet at a party, your friends will likely pressure you to return to your role of the clown. However, if the roles we have assumed are not acceptable to others, they will exert pressure on us to change the roles. For example, if someone assumes the role of a blocker and constantly refuses

to accept anyone's new ideas, other people may exert pressure on the blocker to change that behavior, perhaps by saying, "You always disagree," or "Why don't you listen to what others have to say?" The individual portraying the blocker will usually change his or her behavior, because it is unacceptable to those with whom he or she interacts.

This same process of role adjustment occurs within the small group. In a small group, a role is a function—such as leader, follower, or blocker—assumed by a participant. Each group member may assume one or more roles. Once these roles are assumed, group members may exert pressure on each individual to retain or abandon the roles each has assumed. Let's look at some cases.

Case

Elizabeth had just left her psychology class and was walking toward the student union where she was scheduled to join some friends. Elizabeth was usually very open and talkative. Today, however, she was depressed due to her failing grade on a recent psychology test. Nevertheless, Elizabeth thought a trip to the union and conversation with friends would take her mind off the poor grade. When she arrived at the union, Elizabeth's friends were involved in conversation. After a while, one of her friends said, "Why don't you say something, Elizabeth? You always have something to say." Other friends also asked Elizabeth to talk, but she was unwilling to join the conversation because of her depression. Finally, someone said, "Why don't you leave? You obviously have nothing to offer." As Elizabeth angrily returned to her dorm, she wondered why her friends would not accept her being quiet and withdrawn from the group.

(a) Why did Elizabeth's friends exert pressure on her to talk?

(b) If Elizabeth became a member of a small group, would other members exert pressure on her to be a talkative member? Explain your answer.

- - - - - - - - - - - - - - - - - -

(a) She had always talked before, so the group expected her to continue in that role.
(b) Yes. If Elizabeth began with the group as a talkative person and suddenly became quiet, the group would probably pressure her to talk. However, if the group did not approve of Elizabeth's frequent talking, they might reinforce her silence, encouraging her to assume a quieter role.

3.   Let's look at another case:

Case

Bill, a member of Sigma Wu Fraternity, was quite active in the fraternity's rush program. One Monday afternoon, Bill asked several of his fraternity brothers to join him as he thought of new ideas for the fall rush program. Bill indicated that he wanted them to offer any suggestions they had concerning rush. Mitch suggested a fall party for all students interested in joining Sigma Wu. Gary shouted, "That's a stupid idea. How would we know who was interested?" Bill and the other fraternity men looked at Gary disapprovingly. Bill suggested that Gary find a better way to voice his criticism. Gary then sat down and was far less aggressive with his future criticisms.

(a) Who assumed the unacceptable role?

(b) What kind of group pressure forced this member to change his behavior?

- - - - - - - - - - - - - - - - - -

(a) Gary assumed the unacceptable role.
(b) The negative eye contact from other group members and Bill's suggestion
     that Gary find a more acceptable way to voice his criticism.

4.   If Gary, in the above example, were a member of your small group, would you exert pressure on him to change his behavior? Explain.

- - - - - - - - - - - - - - - - - -

Probably, yes. Gary's behavior would be annoying to group members, and, therefore, most people would pressure him to change.

5.   People often play different roles in different groups because of the differing expectations of the group membership. For example, one group may expect someone to be the leader, while in another group they might expect that some person to be a follower. Look at Sean's experience.

Case 1

Sean was a brilliant high school student scoring in the 99th percentile of his Scholastic Aptitude Test. Members of the Honor Society therefore expected Sean to assume leadership responsibility. Sean, responding to the group's expectations, did become leader of the high school Honor Society.

Case 2
Sean was also asked to be a member of the Social Planning Committee of the
high school. The group wanted Sean to be a member so that he might represent
the social desires of the school's Honor Society. The student body president
was also on the committee, and the group expected her to be the leader since
she represented the entire student body.

In which situation was Sean responding to group expectations? _____

- - - - - - - - - - - - - - - - - - - -

both

6.   Let's look at another case.

Case
After several years at Longview Manufacturing Company, Bill Harris was pro-
moted to production manager. Bill had always wanted the opportunity to introduce changes into the structure of the production group, and he felt his new job
would give him that opportunity. When Bill began his new job, he informed
several of his superiors that he intended to make some changes. They did not
seem particularly pleased with Bill's ideas, but he went ahead with them any-
way.
   On the day Bill began making structural changes, he was called into a
meeting with four of his immediate supervisors. At the meeting Bill sensed
his bosses were displeased with the implementation of the new ideas, but he
was surprised that they did not directly say that they disapproved of his changes.
Rather, they indicated their disapproval in subtle, indirect ways. They discussed how much they liked their jobs and that they hoped Bill enjoyed his as
well. The also suggested that people who want to continue with Longview should
not rock the boat. Before the session ended, Bill realized that his superiors
had delivered a clear message: "Leave well enough alone and you'll keep your
job; otherwise, you have no guarantees." Bill responded to their implied request and suggested no further changes.

(a) What did Bill's supervisors want him to do?

(b) How did Bill's supervisors encourage him not to introduce changes into
     Longview's structure?

(c) What sort of role did Bill's superiors force him to play?

- - - - - - - - - - - - - - - - -

(a) They wanted him to leave well enough alone—not to introduce changes in
     the organization.

(b) They suggested (in a subtle way) that Bill would be unable to retain his job.

(c) a submissive role

THE LEADERSHIP ROLE

7. As we have seen, group members may assume a variety of roles in a small group. One important role is that of leadership.

One of the most important characteristics of the group leader is effective listening. The individual assuming the leadership role should listen carefully on a verbal as well as a nonverbal level. Carl Rogers suggests that we should listen to the total person, not merely to the person's words. For example, a group member may say "I agree" about a certain position, while that member's nonverbal cues may indicate "No, I don't agree." The leader must watch for such nonverbal cues in order to insure adequate representation of the group's opinions. The leader should be careful not to interrupt members who are discussing pertinent issues and should give each speaker undivided attention. In this way, each member will feel a sense of worth and importance. Listening is very important to anyone in the leadership role.

Another responsibility of the individual assuming the leadership role is that of giving orders and offering direction to group members. Often group members may be unaware of specific items or areas of concern to be investigated. During the course of a discussion, a member may say, "I'm confused. I don't know exactly what I should do next." The group leader must be well enough informed to direct the participant to the appropriate areas for discussion.

The group leader must also be capable of stimulating and developing action by group members. After a group has met several times, its labors often become frustrating, and its members may become discouraged. The effective group leader finds it beneficial to encourage group members and to offer continuing assurance that their efforts are appreciated.

In addition, the effective group leader must make sure the group's ideas have been thought through clearly. Sometimes a group will be in a hurry to arrive at a decision and so may settle for superficial ideas. The leader must therefore be capable of questioning the ideas of group members. The leader, for example, may ask, "Have you thought about other issues affecting your position?" or "Will there be any exceptions to the rules you are imposing?" Such provoking questions may greatly assist group members in their efforts to arrive at the very best decisions.

The effective group leader will also be substantially guiding the group as it proceeds. When the group appears to have investigated all aspects of the project, the group leader may need to guide the group in other directions in need of investigation. The group leader may sometimes need to guide the direction of the discussion, especially when the discussion wanders from the real issue. For example, the leader may say, "We seem to have lost track of the major issues. Let's get back to our topic." The leader should therefore constantly be attempting to guide the discussion toward a successful investigation of the issues.

The effective leader will also be <u>evaluating</u> comments and suggestions offered by group members. The leader must exercise caution so as not to offend group members, but he or she must react to what is being said. For example, if a group member indicates that he or she does not feel the group should do research on the project, the leader may have to indicate that research is essential if the proper information is to be gathered. The leader should evaluate the ideas of individual group members as well as the ideas of the total group. Hopefully, all group members will assist the leader in evaluating ideas presented by fellow group members. In any case, the leader must assume the role of evaluator.

The effective group leader must also be capable of <u>summarizing</u>. This function is one key to productive meetings. Often, as a discussion proceeds, members repeat the same ideas. The group leader should say something like, "Let's summarize what has been said and then move forward with the discussion." Such a comment often leads the group into more productive discussion.

Finally, the group leader will be <u>initiating</u> ideas. A leader must be creative and capable of generating thought among the group members. For example, if the group is attempting to find solutions to problems, the group leader may say, "Let me suggest four or five possibilities." Others in the group should be encouraged to do the same. If a group is attempting to raise money for a project, the leader may suggest a variety of ways for the group to accomplish its task and call for other ideas from the group. The leader must generate thought and ideas among the group members.

These eight characteristics are among the most important for those in the leadership role: listening, giving orders and directions, stimulating and developing action, questioning, guiding, evaluating, summarizing, and initiating ideas. Look at the following case and see when each of the eight characteristics is shown. Then answer the questions at the end of the case.

Case

A group of math majors met to decide what suggestions they would make concerning the math curriculum at the University of Arkansas. John, a senior math student, was appointed chairman of the group. He began the first meeting by suggesting all sorts of new ideas for changes in the curriculum. He also suggested that students should have more input into course selection and that certain courses should be eliminated. The introduction of John's suggestions for change really got the group interested; members seemed genuinely concerned with what was happening. The group discussed each of John's suggestions, along with other suggestions from the group. After each suggestion had been discussed, the discussion became repetitive. At this point John suggested that the group wrap up the discussion of these issues and move on to others. Before moving on, he indicated the major points that had been covered and briefly reviewed what had been said about each.

With this, the group moved forward to discuss other critical issues. Larry, a group member, suggested that all math requirements be eliminated. He further suggested that all students be allowed to choose their own courses. John thanked Larry for his ideas but indicated that his suggestions simply would not work because of the north-central evaluating committee's requirement that certain courses be required of all students.

At the third meeting, John began giving each member certain responsibilities. He assigned Mary to search the literature in other college catalogues;
Larry was to interview faculty members in the math department; Cindy was
given the responsibility of interviewing math students; and Wayne was asked
to interview the college administrators. When this material was collected,
the group was to meet again to discuss its findings. After three weeks, the
group met to compare notes. Each member was allocated time to discuss his
or her findings. While each member was speaking, John established excellent
contact with the speaker. He paid close attention to each word and watched
carefully for any nonverbal signs that would further indicate the speaker's state
of mind. Such an attitude on John's part seemed to encourage other members
to enter the discussion. At the conclusion of each report, the group discussed
the member's findings. During the discussion, a couple of members began
talking about the fraternity dance to be held on campus. John indicated that
the discussion was interesting but really did not pertain to the issue. The
group then returned to the subject under consideration.

After several group meetings, the group appeared rather tired of the entire project. Little discussion occurred, and each member seemed eager to
adjourn. John, recognizing the negative attitude of the group members, reminded them all of the work they had done and stressed what a great job they
were doing. In addition, he reminded them that their conclusions could change
the entire philosophy of the math department. When John finished talking, the
group seemed eager once again to continue its efforts.

As the group members began to complete their task, they met to discuss
their findings concerning the math department. During the course of the discussion, John inquired several times about specific issues presented. Because of these frequent inquiries, the group realized several areas remained
to be discussed.

Can you identify the eight leadership characteristics in this case? Describe what was occurring in the case when each characteristic was observable.

(a) Initiating ideas:

(b) Listening:

(c) Giving orders and directions:

(d) Stimulating and developing action:

(e) Questioning:

(f)   Guiding:

(g)   Evaluating:

(h)   Summarizing:

- - - - - - - - - - - - - - - - - - -

(a)   At the first meeting, to get the ball rolling, John suggested many new ideas to the group.
(b)   As each group member reported his or her findings, John listened carefully on both a verbal and nonverbal level.
(c)   John gave each member certain responsibilities and tasks to complete and for the group to discuss.
(d)   When the group became tired of the project, John reminded them of the good work they had done and of their responsibility for potential changes in the math department.
(e)   During one of the final meetings, John's inquiries showed the group that several areas remained to be discussed.
(f)   When a couple of members began discussing a fraternity dance, John asked them to return to the subject.
(g)   When Larry suggested that all math requirements be dropped, John explained why that was impossible.
(h)   When each issue seemed to be thoroughly discussed, John summarized the discussion and suggested moving on to other issues.

GROUP TASK ROLES

8.   As we discussed earlier, leadership is only one of many roles in the group process.   One major classification of roles is the group task roles which are important in achieving productivity.*   Nine different group task roles may be assumed by group members.   Not all group task roles may be present in any one group; a group may function very well with only two group task roles assumed by members.   Remember that one person may assume more than one role.   Generally, however, an individual will identify most closely with one definite role.   That is, while a group member may perform functions required of several roles, his or her primary responsibility will center around one particular role.

---

*Our classification of roles has been adapted from Kenneth D. Benne and Paul Sheates, "Functional Roles of Group Members," The Journal of Social Issues, Vol. IV, No. 2 (Spring 1948), pp. 41-49.

Why is it important to know about group task roles? Knowledge of group task roles can make you a more effective group member. If your group is having problems achieving productivity, the problem may be that some group task roles are not being assumed by members. You can analyze the group and its problems to see whether you or other group members should assume some necessary group task roles. Once the responsibilities inherent in these roles are assumed, the group may become more productive. The nine group task roles are:

Information seeker	Coordinator
Information giver	Orienter
Opinion giver	Energizer
Opinion seeker	Initiator
Clarifier	

Let's examine the nine group task roles, with examples to show their value to the small-group discussion process.

The first of the group task roles is that of the <u>information seeker</u>. A group member assuming this role accepts a very important responsibility. Usually, he or she is a critical thinker who analyzes situations carefully. When information is presented within the group, the information seeker asks for elaboration about the areas investigated and suggests other areas to explore. Do not confuse the information seeker with the person who asks questions merely to obstruct the group process. The information seeker genuinely wants the information in order to assist the group in achieving its goal. The information seeker is particularly valuable in a group which tends to accept information without question. We all need our ideas questioned and discussed. Only in this way do we finally achieve the most effective answers to our questions.

A second important group task role is that of the <u>information giver</u>. Unless carefully researched ideas are presented and discussed, a group is unlikely to arrive at very effective conclusions. The information giver supplies necessary facts and other data concerning the group's project. The information giver may also supply information from personal experience or ideas concerning certain issues. Such information may also be of great value. As we discussed earlier, however, the group must carefully distinguish information based upon research and experience from that based upon feelings. Both types of information are important and worthy of the group's concern, but the group is wise not to let personal feelings, without supporting information and research, unduly affect their decision.

The <u>opinion giver</u> is closely related to the information giver. The most significant difference between the two roles is that the opinion giver offers personal reactions to statements or other issues being discussed without any supporting factual information. The opinion giver serves a vital purpose. Unless each group member feels free to say, "It is my opinion that this policy will never work," a group will have no basis for discussion and thus no basis for further research. In some groups, the group members seem to have no opinions at all. Such a circumstance generally indicates that other problems exist with the group—perhaps the members are shy and feel uncomfortable in sharing their ideas. The result is often catastrophic for the group. If members have not shared their ideas and opinions, the final group decision will not reflect the group's best efforts. If just one group member begins offering an opinion about the matter under discussion, other members will often join in, and discussion generally will become more productive.

The person who asks for the opinions of fellow group members is called the opinion seeker. This person is valuable in encouraging group members—especially quiet members—to participate in the group effort. By seeking the quiet person's opinion, the opinion seeker may create more interaction among all group members. By encouraging the free expression of everyone's opinions, the opinion seeker helps assure that the group's final product represents the thoughts and opinions of all group members.

Another group task role is referred to as the clarifier. Often group members will present ideas that are perfectly clear to them but ambiguous to others. The person who acts as clarifier tries to insure that everyone understands the discussion by offering examples and illustrations of what is being said. For example, if a lay person were asked to join a group of physicians debating expansion of the local hospital, one of the physicians might describe or illustrate why more intensive-care equipment is needed. The clarifier simply helps others to understand what is being discussed.

The group coordinator is an important group task role assumed by a person who is interested in showing relationships among comments, facts, and opinions. For example, during the course of a discussion the group coordinator might say, "What you are saying, Jim, relates closely to the facts presented by Tom last week." This particular role is valuable for the group leader, as well as members of the group, to assume. The coordinator is often the individual who draws a picture demonstrating where each part fits. Such an individual can save valuable time for the group. Instead of allowing the group to discuss certain issues over and over, the coordinator can show relationships among ideas and thus suggest that the group move on to other areas of concern.

Once in a while a group will wander away from the topic being considered. As we have seen, some small talk, joking, and other unrelated discussion is valuable to the group, because it relaxes the members and encourages all to participate. When such unrelated discussion becomes frequent, however, the group is obviously neglecting the major reason for its existence. The group member assuming the group task role of orienter attempts to channel the group group's discussion into the appropriate areas. If the group continues to get off the topic, the orienter reminds the other group members of their purpose and suggests that they return to serious discussion. Thus, the group orienter can save the group many hours otherwise spent in frivolous discussion.

Another group task role is that of the energizer, a person who is concerned that the group continue to work and ultimately perform its task. Group members occasionally become frustrated with their tasks and stop putting in the effort necessary to achieve group productivity. Most groups need someone to assume the energizer role. This individual encourages group action while also encouraging individual group members to contribute their very best efforts.

A final group task role is that of the initiator. The person assuming this role offers suggestions and new ideas about how the group could consider problems or solutions, thus preventing the group from taking a narrow view of the problem or the possible solutions.

All of these group task roles are valuable to the group as the members attempt to accomplish their objective. Not all of these roles need be present for a group to achieve its goals, but in successful groups, most of the group task roles have been assumed by the members. If your group is having difficulty in achieving its goal, perhaps the group task roles have not been assumed. If so, suggest to group members that certain of the task roles need to be assumed for your group to be successful. To test your understanding of group task roles, see if you can correctly answer the following true or false questions.

_____ (a) A group member assumes only one group task role.

_____ (b) In all groups, the nine group task roles are represented.

_____ (c) Those assuming the group task roles generally disrupt the group process.

_____ (d) Those groups in which the nine group task roles are not represented may have difficulty in achieving their objectives.

- - - - - - - - - - - - - - - - - - -

(a) false; (b) false; (c) false; (d) true

9. During a recent meeting of the board of directors of Junction Corporation, the chairman asked if anyone had any new ideas concerning the new product soon to be introduced. Several members volunteered ideas. Finally, Eric indicated that several of the ideas were related to one another. He explained the relationship he observed among the ideas and suggested that the group expand upon the related ideas.

What group task role did Eric assume? Explain.

- - - - - - - - - - - - - - - - - -

Coordinator. Eric showed the relationship among the various ideas presented by the group.

10. The President's Council of Economic Advisors met to discuss what could be done about the inflation problem in the United States. The chairperson called the meeting to order. Sam requested that the other panel members put aside all the data and facts and simply report their feelings and reactions to the situation. Each of the economic advisors complied with Sam's request. Several noted, however, that they were simply reporting their observations and feelings; they were not necessarily in compliance with the facts of the situation indicated.

(a) What group task role did Sam assume? Explain.

(b) What group task role did the economic advisors assume? Explain.

- - - - - - - - - - - - - - - - - - -

(a) Opinion seeker. Sam is asking for feelings about the issues.
(b) Opinion givers. The ideas expressed are related to their feelings, not
     necessarily to the facts surrounding the issues.

11. The Campus Review Board was scheduled to meet in the student union at
4:00 p.m. on Friday. Many of its members had been absent from previous
meetings, and Bryan, the chairman, hoped that all members would be present
at this one. Fortunately, all members arrived on time, and the meeting began
as scheduled. As the meeting progressed, however, the members began discussing everything except the issues confronting the group. Finally Max, a
group member, suggested that the group return to its intended purpose and
discuss the issues requiring its attention. With Max's urging, the group returned to its assigned task.

What group task role did Max assume? Explain.

- - - - - - - - - - - - - - - - - - -

Group orienter. Max asked the group to return to the topic under discussion.

12. The city of Nashville was having difficulty finding solutions to a very serious pollution problem. The mayor decided to appoint a committee to study
the problem and to suggest solutions. The mayor appointed four engineers
who specialized in the reduction of air pollution and two concerned individuals
from the community who had little academic understanding of air pollution.
At the third meeting, one of the engineers began discussing the ozone level
and the effects air pollution would have on this critical layer of our atmosphere.
The two lay members obviously did not understand what was being said. Finally, Alan, one of the engineers, drew some diagrams on the board and gave
some examples of the effects of air pollution on the ozone belt.

What group task role did Allan assume? Explain.

- - - - - - - - - - - - - - - - - - -

Clarifier. He explained the issues to group members who did not understand.

13. Fran was a member of a group originally established to investigate possible solutions for the campus parking problem. Although the group was very concerned about the problem, its members were slow to act. At one meeting, Cindy stood and exclaimed, "We have got to act now! Recent statistics show that the campus problems are increasing." She encouraged each member to do his or her best job in arriving at the solutions.

What group task role did Cindy assume? Explain.

- - - - - - - - - - - - - - - - -

Energizer. She encouraged the group to take action.

14. A group of Vietnam veterans held a series of meetings to determine what should be done to assist unemployed veterans. Jake related his personal frustrations in trying to get a job and also provided factual data concerning sixty other veterans who experienced similar frustrations in job-seeking.

What group task role did Jake assume? Explain.

- - - - - - - - - - - - - - - - -

Information giver. Jake provided factual data concerning himself and sixty other veterans.

15. As the meeting of the veterans continued, it became apparent that more investigation was required. The group simply did not have enough background to recommend solutions. Wayne, the chairman, assigned individuals within the group specific tasks to perform. Each member was required to gather specific factual data to assist the group in eventually arriving at its decision.

Besides the leadership role, what other group task role did Wayne assume? Explain.

- - - - - - - - - - - - - - - - -

Information seeker. Wayne assigned each member the responsibility of gathering more information.

16. Jo Ann was asked to join a group considering the elimination of the traditional grading system at the University of California. When she joined the group, the other members had been meeting for several weeks. Jo Ann realized that the group had been discussing the problems of grades for some time, but she felt that the group had neglected to consider the effects a new grading

system would have on students who sought entrance to graduate schools. Jo Ann introduced this potential problem, and the group members agreed that they had not considered it as part of the grading question. They expressed their gratitude to Jo Ann and sought solutions to the problem she had raised.

What group task role did Jo Ann assume? Explain.

- - - - - - - - - - - - - - - - - -

Initiator. Jo Ann suggested new ideas and thus prompted the group to further discussion.

GROUP BUILDING-AND-MAINTENANCE ROLES

17. As noted at the beginning of this chapter, we all play a variety of roles in our daily lives. Some of the roles we play in small groups serve a constructive purpose, while others are destructive. The group task roles we have just discussed serve a constructive purpose. The second classification of group roles—group building and maintenance roles—also support group solidarity and productivity. Individuals assuming the group building and maintenance roles are concerned with establishing good interpersonal relations while encouraging the group to function together. Remember that a group member may assume one or more roles but will usually be most comfortable with one particular role. The four group building and maintenance roles we will discuss in this section are:

Supporter	Tension reliever
Harmonizer	Gate keeper

These roles are very important to group productivity. Without effective interpersonal relationships, problems become impossible to solve. In the small group setting, the more important a member feels, the more useful his or her contribution is likely to be. Effective interpersonal relationships are also necessary to ensure adequate representation from all group members; if relationships are striained, members will probably not give their best efforts, causing group productivity to suffer. As with the group task roles, not all the group building and maintenance roles need to be present for a group to be successful. If your group is having difficulty, however, analyze the roles assumed by group members. Perhaps part of the group's problem is that no one is assuming the group building and maintenance roles. If so, you may be able to encourage group members to adopt these.

The first group building and maintenance role is that of the group supporter. For a group to be cohesive, each person must feel that he or she is an important member, making significant contributions to the group. The group supporter helps insure solidarity by praising group members for their efforts. This does not mean that the group supporter offers encouragement for mediocre work. If we receive compliments for work poorly done, we soon lose confidence in the person offering the compliments. The supporter is a group member who recognizes good work and compliments the appropriate person. Such recognition encourages further good work.

The second group building and maintenance role is that of the <u>harmonizer</u>. Occasionally, group members experience some sort of conflict. The conflict may occur between just two group members or among all the group members. Such conflict need not be serious and may in fact reflect a closely united group. (Remember that in groups with much tension, most members feel reluctant to discuss issues freely, so little, if any, conflict occurs. As a result, ideas are often accepted too quickly, when some conflict or arguments might have led to a more thorough analysis of the problems.) Most productive groups do experience conflict, which can be constructive if it does not continue over a long period of time. The person assuming the role of harmonizer assists in resolving interpersonal conflicts by helping the members view their situation objectively. Usually, the harmonizer is acutely aware of nonverbal cues indicating that an individual member feels conflict concerning some aspect of the group's activity. One group member may be angry at another and yet chose to say nothing, instead withdrawing from the group. An observant harmonizer may notice nonverbal cues from the angry person and at an appropriate time ask if his or her observations of the conflict are accurate. If so, the harmonizer attempts to have the conflicting parties state their grievances and work toward finding solutions to their problems.

Another important group building and maintenance role is that of the <u>tension reliever</u>. Tensions often build in a group, and members seek constructive avenues for the release of these tensions. The tension reliever is a person who is able to relax the group members, helping them release their tensions and return to the group's task. Often this tension relief takes the form of joking and relating humorous incidents from the group's past. As we all know, when we experience tension and frustrations, we do not function at full capacity. The tension reliever is therefore a very important person. The role of tension reliever is most often assumed by someone who frequently makes people laugh.

A final group building and maintenance role is that of the <u>gatekeeper</u>. The individual assuming the gatekeeper's role encourages the quiet members of the group to communicate. The gatekeeper may also encourage the more vocal members to give other members a chance to voice their opinions. If one or two members within your group remain quiet throughout the discussion, the final group product or decision will not represent the entire group. The gatekeeper doesn't pester people to communicate or get involved; such behavior may in fact discourage people. Rather the gatekeeper asks for member contributions when appropriate. For example, if all the group members but one have discussed a certain issue, the gatekeeper may ask for the opinion of the remaining member. The gatekeeper also may explain to that member why his or her participation is so important. Hopefully, such gatekeeping behavior will encourage all members to participate.

Now that you have read a description of the group building and maintenance roles, see if you can identify them in the following examples. Recall the four group building and maintenance roles: supporter, harmonizer, tension reliever, and gatekeeper.

Case

At a group meeting, several lawyers were discussing local zoning ordinances. It soon became obvious that they disagreed on an important issue involving city zoning. Paula, a group member, interjected a humorous incident involving a neighboring community and their problems with the zoning ordinances. The members enjoyed the story and became more relaxed as they continued at the task.

What group building and maintenance role did Paula assume?

- - - - - - - - - - - - - - - - - -

tension reliever

18. A group of six sorority women met to decide whether one of the recent pledges should be allowed to become an active member of the sorority. Maria absolutely refused to discuss the matter. She indicated that she distrusted the pledge and did not want her as a sorority sister. Freda indicated that Maria was absolutely wrong and should not be allowed to make such damaging remarks against the pledge. The two began to argue and refused to consider each other's viewpoint. Jenny stopped the argument and suggested that Freda and Maria apologize to each other and begin discussing the matter rationally.

What group building and maintenance role did Jenny assume?

- - - - - - - - - - - - - - - - - -

harmonizer

19. A local church group met to discuss the financial crisis confronting many poor families in the community. All members, with the exception of Paul, contributed ideas to the group. Mary, seeing that Paul was quiet, began asking Paul for his opinion. Soon Paul assumed an active part in the group.

What group building and maintenance role did Mary assume?

- - - - - - - - - - - - - - - - - -

gatekeeper

20. Jane has been an airline flight attendant for six years. Because of her many experiences, she was asked by her supervisor to join a group of beginning flight attendants. The group's purpose was to discuss potential problems and to propose solutions. Jane realized that the beginning flight attendants were experiencing tension due to their lack of experience and their desire to do a good job. She therefore praised the ideas offered by the flight attendants.

Jane's encouragement seemed to relax the new employees so they were able to establish credible solutions to their problems.

What group building and maintenance role did Jane assume?

- - - - - - - - - - - - - - - - - -

supporter

21. Now let's see how well you recognize these group building and maintenance roles as they interact.

Case
A group of airline pilots met to discuss the problem of air piracy and what could be done about solving the problem. Seven pilots were involved in the discussion. Bill began by suggesting that people convicted of air piracy should be executed. Harold (1) praised Bill's suggestion and indicated that he was inclined to agree with Bill, but he also wanted to hear the suggestions of the other men. As other suggestions were voiced, Harold praised the pilots for their good ideas. Suddenly, Tom demanded to know where Jake's "ridiculous suggestion" came from. Jake retorted with, "My suggestion is no more ridiculous than yours." The two men continued to argue until Fred (2) suggested that both men had a contribution to make and that one was no better than the other. Jim (3) interjected a funny story about an occurence on a recent flight. Everyone laughed and enjoyed the story and each man seemed more relaxed as a result. Finally, Frank (4) observed that Jim had not said very much and encouraged him to voice his opinion, which he did.

(a) What group building and maintenance role did Harold (1) assume?

(b) What group building and maintenance role did Fred (2) assume?

(c) What group building and maintenance role did Jim (3) assume?

(d) What group building and maintenance role did Frank (4) assume?

- - - - - - - - - - - - - - - - - -

(a) supporter; (b) harmonizer; (c) tension reliever; (d) gatekeeper

SELF-CENTERED ROLES

22. The last category of roles assumed by group members is the self-centered roles. Unlike group task roles and the group building and maintenance roles, the self-centered roles are destructive to the group discussion process. These roles are characterized by behaviors that satisfy individual needs at the group's expense. Such behavior severely hinders the group's productivity. Group members should be alert to recognize and discourage self-centered roles

among their fellow group members. If someone has assumed a self-centered role, indicate to that member the destructive potential of that behavior and suggest that he or she change for the benefit of the group.

The first of the self-centered roles is that of the blocker. We have all met this individual in either a one-to-one conversation or a small group. As we attempt to communicate, we find the blocker constantly raising objections to issues being discussed, insisting that nothing can be done about a problem, or returning to issues that have already been discussed. Such behavior can make the rest of the group defensive, causing members to neglect the completion of the group's task. This does not mean that any group member who objects to the issues being discussed is assuming the role of the blocker. Such objections can be a real benefit to the group. The blocker, however, objects indiscriminately and obstructs the group's movement toward the completion of its task. Again, to keep your group effective, you must inform the blocker of the destructive nature of that behavior and ask him or her to assume more constructive group behavior. Those who continue in the blocker's role may eventually be requested to leave, so the group's work at its task will not suffer.

A second self-centered role is that of the aggressor. This role is assumed by a person who deflates the status of others, expresses disapproval, or jokes at the expense of others. Such a person might say, for example, "You have not had nearly enough experience in this area. How would you know what you're talking about?" The aggressor may even tell jokes embarrassing to group members, often causing the victim to shy away from commenting on issues confronting the group. When this occurs, the group fails to function at its full capacity. The aggressor should be told that the behavior is destructive and be asked to change for the benefit of the entire group.

Another self-centered role is that of the recognition seeker. Such people spend most of their time in the group boasting about themselves or relating irrelevant personal experiences. For example, the recognition seeker may say about the topic being discussed, "Oh yes, that reminds me of when I..." This "I-centered" person will do anything possible to turn the discussion in his or her direction. This person impedes the group discussion process and should be discouraged from doing so.

See if you can identify the blocker, aggressor, and recognition seeker in the following case:

Case

A group of concerned citizens met to discuss the critical power shortage in the United States. Dan established criteria for the group, while May suggested that group members invite experts to speak to them about the problem. Jerry (1) indicated that he had probably read more than any other member about the power shortage. In fact, he said he doubted that few, if any, people in America had read as much as he. Larry (2) thanked Jerry for his contribution and agreed with him; he indicated that several people in the group had little real education and were probably incapable of reading. Cindy (3) agreed and suggested that the group disband because they could do nothing to solve the problem. Other members refused; they remained behind and continued their discussion.

(a)   What self-centered role did Jerry (1) assume?

(b)   What self-centered role did Larry (2) assume?

(c)   What self-centered role did Cindy (3) assume?

- - - - - - - - - - - - - - - - - -

(1) recognition seeker; (b) aggressor; (c) blocker

23. Three other self-centered roles include those of the confessor, the dominator, and the special-interest pleader.

The role assumed by an individual who uses the group as an audience for
personal ill feelings, mistakes, attitudes, and beliefs is the <u>confessor</u>. Most
of us have met people who play the confessor. Often the confessor will discuss
subjects foreign to the group's topic. For example, when the group is discussing foreign policy, the confessor may begin talking about his or her poor in-
vestments or bad feelings about financial consultants. When this occurs, the
group discussion process is obstructed, and the completion of the group task
is delayed. The confessor should be advised of the adverse effects of this behavior and asked to remain within the confines of the group topic.

The role of the <u>dominator</u> is characterized by a desire to lead the group
by ordering members about and insisting that the discussion be conducted in
a certain way. Thus, the dominator also impedes the group discussion process. Frequently, the group has not given power to the dominator; rather,
the dominator demands power. The dominator also attempts to talk more than
other group members, often discouraging shy members from participating.
Most group members respond negatively to the dominator and consequently do
not exert as much individual effort toward the group's function. The dominator should be requested to alter his or her behavior. Otherwise, the group
may have to reject the dominator from the group.

A final self-centered role—that of the <u>special interest pleader</u>—is assumed
by someone who is interested in representing another group. Although the
special-interest pleader is a member of one group, he or she really owes allegiance to another. For example, if an insurance salesman were a member
of a group whose task was to formulate insurance policies for Medicare, he
might serve as a special-interest pleader, perhaps interjecting comments such
as, "We can't do that—the salesmen would go broke." In that case, the insurance salesman would be pleading for the interests of salesmen, nor for effective Medicare policies. This individual would be obstructing the group discussion process by pleading a special interest.

Now see if you can recognize the last three roles—confessor, dominator,
and special-interest pleader—in the following case.

Case
A group of scientists gathered to discuss the future of the space program in
the United States. Several issues had been discussed when Jan (1) began

discussing the mistakes he had made when he first began seeking a job. The rest of the group listened politely. Finally, they got the discussion back to the major issues confronting the future of the space program. Bart (2) insisted that the members should concentrate on the twenty-first century in their discussion; he subsequently began ordering other members to begin researching in specific major areas of concern. Members objected to Jake's obvious attempt to control the group. Once again, the members returned to discussing the issues involved with the space program. Martha (3) interrupted, indicating that she represented the Ecology Foundation; she insisted that all space exploration should be terminated because of damage to the environment. The group members indicated that they would be glad to discuss the issue at another meeting. Again the group returned to its original function.

(a) What self-centered role did Jan (1) assume?

(b) What self-centered role did Bart (2) assume?

(c) What self-centered role did Martha (3) assume?

- - - - - - - - - - - - - - - - - - -

(a) confessor; (b) dominator; (c) special-interest pleader

SUMMARY

In Chapter 5, we have explored how roles in group discussion are positions occupied by group members. The patterns of behavior associated with these roles can assist or block group members in their problem-solving efforts. Group task roles and group building and maintenance roles are supportive and essential to group productivity. Self-centered roles are destructive. We have seen how the leadership role, to be effective, requires certain important and distinct patterns of behavior.

SELF-TEST

The following questions will help you assess how well you understand the material in Chapter 5. Answer the questions, and then look at the answers and review instructions that follow.

Part A

In this chapter we have discussed three general classifications of roles: group task roles, group building and maintenance roles, and self-centered roles. This final case will involve all of the roles we have discussed. See if you can recognize all of the roles. If you have a problem, review the appropriate part of the chapter.

Case

A small commercial jet carrying thirty passengers including the crew, crashed into the Atlantic Ocean. Fortunately, all survived the crash and, after many fearful and frustrating moments, found themselves safely aboard the life raft. Within a few hours, they had drifted far away from the crash site. The captian of the plane and his crew continued to reassure the crash victims that they would be rescued.

One of the passengers, Roy (1) praised all of the crew and passengers for the way they had conducted themselves after the crash. He indicated that no one would have survived had they not all cooperated. Tony (2), one of the pilots, agreed with Roy and he, too, complimented his fellow crew members and the passengers on their conduct after the crash. He then suggested that he present necessary information dealing with rescue procedures. Helen (3), another passenger, interrupted Tony and said that her husband had been a pilot and she knew exactly what to do; she began giving everyone orders and directions that she remembered from her husband's conversations. Grant explained to Helen that the flight crew was better suited to give the necessary information. All agreed with Grant. As a result, Helen was angry and obviously quite upset. Pat (4), observing Helen's mood, asked and received permission to tell a short funny story. When she had finished, Helen and the rest of the passengers seemed to be in better spirits.

Tony went on to present the necessary instructions, but when he finished, many of the passengers appeared confused. Bill (5), another crew member, observed the confusion and suggested that he would elaborate on any of the procedures Tony had discussed and would give the group an example of exactly what would happen during rescue operations. When Bill had concluded doing so, Eric (6) indicated that, in his opinion, everything was clear as to the rescue operations. Mary (7), a passenger, said she thought that the explanation was poorly done and that her eight-year-old son could have done better. Other passengers offered to assist in explaining the procedure again to Mary. Josh (8), a passenger, said that Mary was right in being so honest. All channels of communication must remain open, so Mary and all other should feel free to speak out when they were confused.

Suddenly, Kim (9) began complaining about the airline and said they all might as well give up, since nothing could be done about their plight. Susan (10), a flight attendant, disagreed. She proclaimed that everyone needed to develop a sense of security and confidence—they were going to survive. She also suggested that, to take their minds off the present circumstances, the passengers each tell something about themselves. Clyde (11), a passenger, began by telling everyone that he was the most popular member of his community. He boasted about all the awards he had received and all the famous people he had met. Jamey (12), another passenger, suggested that they try a new method of discussing their biographical information. He proposed that each person include the funniest thing that had ever happened to him. Lou (13) asked what Jamey's idea of "funny" was. Jamey explained, and everyone agreed to try his suggestion.

. After several people had spoken, Phil (14) suggested that several definite relationships were apparent among the lives of the passengers and suggested that each person try to integrate his or her ideas with those of a person who had gone before. Ruth (15) was confused by Phil's suggestion and requested additional information. Phil explained his idea and suggested that Betty (16) try it. Instead, she began relating mistakes she had made in her life and delivered a lengthy discourse about her beliefs and feelings concerning the power of the executive branch of government. Troy was upset that Betty had taken so much time and began to argue with her. Judy (17) suggested that both people calm down. She noted that both had something to say and that they should respect each other's rights. Gene (18) agreed and reminded the group members of their purpose, suggesting that they continue their discussion. Dave (19) then resumed the discussion by informing everyone that he did not want to participate; he belonged to a select group of people in New York, and he had absolutely no desire to join in the discussion. He subsequently began explaining about the group to which he belonged. While he was talking, a rescue plane was spotted, and everyone forgot about Dave and his group.

All of the roles we have discussed are listed below. What role is each person from the case (identified by number) assuming?

Group Task Roles	Group Building and Maintenance Roles	Self-Centered Roles
Initiator	Supporter	Blocker
Information seeker	Harmonizer	Aggressor
Information giver	Tension reliever	Recognition seeker
Opinion seeker	Gatekeeper	Confessor
Opinion giver		Dominator
Clarifier		Special-interest pleader
Coordinator		
Orienter		

(1) Roy: _____

(2) Tony: _____

(3) Helen: _____

(4) Pat: _____

(5) Bill: _____

(6) Eric: _____

(7) Mary: _____

(8) Josh: _____

(9) Kim: _____

(10) Susan: _____

(11) Clyde: _____

(12) Jamey: _____

(13) Lou: _____

(14) Phil: _____

(15) Ruth: _____

(16) Betty: _____

(17) Judy: _____

(18) Gene: _____

(19) Dave: _____

Part B

1. What factors determine what roles we play in a group?

2. Can any member assume one or more roles in a given group? Why or why not?

3. Can a person play different roles in different groups? Explain.

4. Compare and contrast group task roles with group building-and-maintenance roles.

5. In this chapter we discussed eight characteristics of an effective leader. Name at least five.

6.   Are self-centered roles destructive to the group process? Why or why not?

Answers to Self-Test

Compare your answers to the questions on the Self-Test with the answers given below. If all your answers are correct, go on to the next chapter. If you had difficulty with any questions, you may want to review the frames indicated in parentheses following the answers. If you missed several questions, you should probably reread the entire chapter carefully.

Part A

(1) Roy: supporter; (2) Tony: information giver; (3) Helen: dominator;
(4) Pat: tension reliever; (5) Bill: clarifier; (6) Eric: opinion giver; (7) Mary: aggressor; (8) Josh: gatekeeper; (9) Kim: blocker; (10) Susan: energizer;
(11) Clyde: recognition seeker; (12) Jamey: initiator; (13) Lou: opinion seeker;
(14) Phil: coordinator; (15) Ruth: information seeker; (16) Betty: confessor;
(17) Judy: harmonizer; (18) Gene: orienter; (19) Dave: special-interest pleader
(frames 8-23)

Part B

1.   The requirements of the situation and the other people involved, as well as our own strengths and weaknesses, determine the role we play in a group. We play a part we desire to play, provided that the other members of the group expect and allow us to play that part in that situation. (frames 1-6)

2.   Yes. We may assume a number of roles in a group over a period of time. Depending upon the needs of the group and our own desires, we may sometimes assume roles essential to the welfare of the group and at other times assume destructive roles, as if a role were a suit of clothes which we put on or take off to suit the occasion. (frames 1-6)

3.   Yes. Because roles are jointly worked out by the individual and the group, a person may assume a leadership role in one group, a group building and maintenance role in another, a task role in a third, and a self-centered role in still another—or any combination in a given group. (frames 1-23)

4.   Group task roles are those that relate directly to the task, as in selection, definition, analysis, appraisal of a problem, and the solution to that

problem. Group building and maintenance roles are oriented more toward the socio-emotional climate of the group; they aid in the alteration or maintenance of the group way of working to strengthen, regulate, and maintain the group as a group. The differences are subtle, however; in reality, the task and social roles are inseparable and interdependent. It is difficult for a group to be productive if its members are not satisfied and, conversely, it is difficult for the members to be satisfied if the group is not productive. (frames 8-21)

5. You should have listed at least five of these leadership characteristics: (a) listening, (b) giving orders and directions, (c) stimulating and developing action, (d) questioning, (e) guiding, (f) evaluating, (g) summarizing, and (h) initiating ideas. (frame 7)

6. Self-centered roles are destructive, because they seek to satisfy individual needs at the group's expense. These roles can severely hinder the group in task accomplishment as well as hurting the group building and maintenance efforts (socio-emotional climate). A preponderance of self-centered roles may suggest a morale problem, a lack of group maturity, a poorly defined task, or inept leadership. (frames 22-23)

CHAPTER SIX

Leadership in
Problem-Solving Discussion

Chapter 5 introduced leadership as one of many roles people assume in discussion groups. Chapter 6 will focus upon specific characteristics and dimensions of leadership and the relationship of leadership to problem-solving group discussion. We will focus especially on leadership emergence, leadership styles, and leadership functions.

OBJECTIVES

When you have completed this chapter, you will be able to:

- Explain the nature of leadership emergence.

- Identify and describe styles of leadership.

- Identify and explain the strengths and weaknesses of different leadership styles.

- Identify voluntary and involuntary factors contributing to leadership emergence.

- Describe and explain procedural and coordinating functions of leadership.

LEADERSHIP EMERGENCE

1. Many factors affect the overall quality, success, and effectiveness of a group discussion and its final product. While leadership is only one of many factors, it is obviously an important one. For our purposes, we define leadership as the exertion of influence and direction over the other members of the group; any group member who exerts such influence will be referred to as a group leader. Group members may become leaders in various ways: They may be appointed by someone outside the group, they may assume leadership due to their office or rank, or they may emerge from among the group.

Situations where appointed leadership occurs are common. If a business organization encounters a problem that cannot be solved by standard corporate procedures or routines, an executive officer of that firm may select several subordinates, appoint one of them leader, and direct this group to solve the problem. A mayor of a large city may appoint a prominent citizen to lead a group which is to find ways to help needy senior citizens pay their utility bills.

Leadership by virtue of office or rank is also common. For example, a person's position in the organizational bureaucracy may require group leadership: A personnel director serves, by right of office, as leader of an employees' benefit committee. The senior member of the Roman Catholic College of Cardinals performs, due to his rank, certain leadership functions when the College of Cardinals meets to elect a new pope.

Emergent leadership is not as clear-cut or as easily defined as appointed or assumed leadership. Emergence of a leader from within the group generally depends upon two sets of factors: first, physical traits or features which the group members cannot directly control, such as physical size, attractiveness, age, and intelligence; second those features which group members can control, such as willingness to work, preparation, contribution of ideas, making a good impression, amount of participation, and seating arrangement.

Physical size is one trait that positively affects leadership emergence. In general, if a person is physically superior to other members in height, weight, or physique, within the range of what is considered "attractive," he or she has a better chance to emerge as the group's leader. This phenomenon may occur because we are an athletically oriented society, because we are subconsciously intimidated by someone larger than we are, or because physically superior people are perceived as more energetic than smaller ones. Whatever the reason, physical size appears to give some members a better chance to become group leaders. The following case demonstrates this principle.

Case
Stella, a maid at Lakewood Lodge, instructed Frances to clean the bathrooms more thoroughly than she had been doing. Frances immediately retorted in an obscene manner and reached for some of Stella's hair. Suddenly, the two women were rolling on the floor clawing at each other. The other maids, looking for leadership in solving the matter, inevitably turned to the largest member of the group, Evelyn. Evelyn ordered the two maids to stop fighting, and they complied immediately.

Why was Evelyn chosen by the group to break up the fight?

- - - - - - - - - - - - - - - - - - - -

because of her size

2. Older members in a group tend to emerge as leaders slightly more often than younger participants. Society encourages us to respect people who are older than we are, so we usually perceive them as having more experience and therefore being more qualified to assume a position of leadership. Not every group selects a leader because of age, but a definite advantage does exist for those members whose age is above the group average.

A third factor that positively affects leadership emergence is physical attractiveness. By attractiveness, we are referring to highly subjective value judgments regarding beauty and appearance, as indicated in such statements as "he looks like a leader" or "her good looks make her a natural leader." Politicians are keenly aware of this factor; since the use of television has become widespread in political campaigns, they have made great efforts to appear attractive, handsome, virile, and so forth.

A fourth factor affecting leadership emergence is intelligence. As the group looks for guidance to solve complex problems, the members who are perceived by the other group members as knowledgable and intelligent are likely to be viewed with respect. Such respect inevitably aids an individual in attempts to emerge as a leader. The following example will help clarify these concepts.

Case

The maids' fight had not gone unnoticed by the management at Lakewood Lodge. The fight was but one more instance of continuing cleaning and maintenance problems. The rooms were not being cleaned properly, and on some occasions the maids were not cleaning certain rooms at all (claiming that they didn't have enough time). To make matters worse, the maids were developing negative attitudes toward any suggestions that advocated a change in their cleaning methods. The board of directors of the lodge decided to meet and discuss some possible solutions to the situation.

Lakewood Lodge was locally owned, but it was affiliated with a nationwide motel chain—Lodge America. Compounding the board's problems was a letter from Lodge America stating that it had received several customer complaints of unkempt and soiled rooms at Lakewood Lodge. If the local board failed to meet the standards set by Lodge America, Lakewood Lodge would lose its franchise. The board of directors of the lodge comprised five people, all of whom were co-owners. Since Frank, board member and lodge manager, lived in the lodge, the meeting was held in his office. Frank had formerly played center for the local high school basketball team and still played for a local semi-pro team. He had not participated in any sports while in college, since he was afraid that such participation might interfere with his studies. In fact, he had been graduated with honors. Frank felt that the problem could be solved by hiring additional maids and service help.

Deborah, slightly older than Frank, had not attended college but had built a very successful real estate business. A diminutive woman, she had certainly never played basketball; she did have striking good looks. She agreed with Frank's position that more maids would help, but she did not want to hire as many as Frank did.

John, small and rotund, favored motivating the present cleaning and maintenance staff through cash bonuses but insisted that any employee who failed to meet the daily work schedule be fired on the spot.

Carol was very withdrawn during the meeting. She had not been an owner very long and didn't know much about the lodge business. It became clear after a few minutes of discussion that she would support any solution offered by the group.

Eric, who was at least thirty years older than the others, agreed that more maids would help but also felt that Lakewood Lodge should hire a maintenance supervisor to direct and oversee the daily maintenance and cleaning duties.

(a) At least four features or traits which an individual has little or no control over contribute to leadership emergence. Name those features or traits.

(b) What traits might contribute to Frank's emerging as leader?

(c) What traits might contribute to Deborah's emerging as leader?

(d) If Eric emerges as the group leader, what trait might be a contributing factor?

(e) Based upon a physical trait or feature approach, would either John or Carol emerge as leader?

- - - - - - - - - - - - - - - - - - - -

(a) physical size, age, attractiveness, intelligence; (b) physical traits (those he had demonstrated as a basketball player) and intelligence; (c) attractiveness, intelligence (shown by her success in business); (d) age; (e) no

3. The second set of features that affect leadership emergence are factors that we can manage. These features include: (1) willingness to work, (2) preparation, (3) contribution of ideas, (4) making a good impression, (5) amount of participation, and (6) seating arrangement. Obviously, other features are involved, but the group member who is able to control these variables enhances his or her chances to emerge as group leader.

The desire to emerge as the leader of the group is a passion felt by many people. Yet people possessing this drive may find themselves receiving instructions from ineffective, domineering, and often less-likable leaders. How does such a leader consistently manage to overshadow others, even when someone else would seem to be more desirable? Perhaps it is because he or she has the greater desire to be the leader. Anyone who wishes to exert leadership influence in a group must demonstrate a willingness to work. Although he or she may not be the most technically qualified member of the group, an emergent leader often is the person best prepared for the group meeting. This individual assumes the leadership role because he or she has made some preparation and is familiar with the topic, has several ideas to contribute, and has a plan of action for the group. The following case illustrates this point.

Case

Merchants in a midwestern college town were experiencing declining sales and profits. The story was much the same as in many other American cities and towns; shopping malls, good roads and highways, suburban housing developments, and a mobile population had reduced the importance of the downtown business district. Compounding the problem was the weekend flight of a substantial portion of the college-student population. In the past, most students had stayed on campus most weekends and had spent their money locally. Now, however, increasing numbers of students owned or had access to cars, and on weekends they went home or drove to a nearby major metropolitan city. Several downtown businesspeople organized an informal meeting to discuss the problem.

Wayne, one of the organizers, stood and addressed the group. "I don't know where to start, and I don't want to run this meeting. From time to time, we've all expressed concern about the situation downtown, so let's talk for a while."

Shawn, a local watch and clock repairman, retorted, "C'mon, Wayne. My business is as good as it ever was." Several other merchants nodded in agreement.

Phil, owner of Phil's Television and Stereo Center, had a different point of view. "What you say, Shawn, is at the heart of the problem. Your business shouldn't be just as good as it ever was. It should be much better. Look here, I have a report from the State Commerce Department showing that, statewise, retail sales are growing four times faster than the rate in our town. I also have data comparing population growth and bank deposits in the community with money spent for products and services, and we're standing still."

Jill, who managed a clothing store, interrupted Phil. "There's not a lot we can do as long as those college students run home every weekend."

Phil answered, "Why do you say that? It sounds like you're content to do the same amount of business year in and year out."

Jill, caught somewhat unprepared, replied, "I don't have any facts on the matter, but it just doesn't seem worth the effort."

Rita, who had been very quiet up to this point, remarked, "I think we can do something, and it will be worth the effort. I'm willing to contribute my time and efforts to see this thing through; if we want to keep the downtown alive, we've got to work at it."

(a) Which participants in the example above are emerging as possible leaders?

(b) What traits or characteristics are contributing to the emergence of this person or these persons?

- - - - - - - - - - - - - - - - - -

(a) Phil and Rita; (b) Phil came to the meeting prepared; Rita expressed willingness to work for the group.

4. Having knowledge about the problem and willingness to work are important
but also important are ideas that shape factual knowledge and give direction to
work. Since the ultimate group goal is to make a decision leading to problem
solution, those members who offer ideas leading to such decisions often emerge
as leaders. A group member's ideas must be perceived by the rest of the
group as being beneficial—not just any idea will do. The following case continues with the downtown merchants' meeting. Take note of the ideas expressed.

Case
"All right, so we're not receiving our share of the business," muttered Shawn,
"but where do we go from here?"

"I have an idea," said Jill. "Why don't we survey all the customers who
come into our stores and ask them what they like about shopping downtown?"

Phil answered, "I'm not sure we need to be overly concerned with the
opinions of those customers who already shop downtown. What we need to know
is why those people who shop elsewhere don't shop downtown."

Rita commented, "I think both Jill and Phil have something to say, but
many other cities have found ways to halt declining downtown business districts.
Wouldn't it be a better use of our time if we visited and studied some of those
cities?"

On the basis of the ideas offered by the group members, which person has
the better chance to emerge as leader? Explain.

- - - - - - - - - - - - - - - - - -

Rita. Rita's idea has more potential. Jill's idea has already been rejected
by Phil, and Phil's idea, while having merit, doesn't go far enough.

5. Groups often select leaders through a process of elimination. To have a
chance to survive the elimination process, an aspiring member must make a
favorable impression on the group very early. Research shows that about one-
half the members are eliminated during the first meeting. People are eliminated if they are quiet, obnoxious, or extreme and inflexible in their beliefs.
During the formation of the group, any group participant who desires leadership is careful to avoid being labeled as an inadequate choice for leader.

Similar to making a good impression is the amount of participation engaged
in by a group member. A member who frequently participates, one who is verbally active, often emerges as the group leader. Unfortunately, available evidence indicates that the quality of comments is not as important as the number
of comments. In other words, a participant who provides a lot of comments,
if they are not viewed as inept, has a better chance to emerge as group leader.
When a group has more than one member who is exceptionally active verbally,
generally competition arises for leadership. When this situation occurs, the
mere act of participation will not guarantee the coveted leadership role. Out-
talking another talkative group member would not be a wise strategy. The

group's goals, values, and needs should be kept paramount over personal wants and desires. When group members are given the choice between a potential leader who is obviously willing to make sacrifices for the sake of the goal and one who merely wants to dominate the discussion, they will probably choose the former. The following example illustrates both making a good impression and active participation.

Case
An unincorporated subdivision located just beyond the city limits was experiencing increasing trouble with stray dogs. While most of the residents viewed themselves as part of the city, city officials could do nothing, because the area was outside the city limits. Appeals had also been made to the county sheriff, who claimed that lack of funds and manpower prevented "dog patrols." After all, the sheriff had stated in a recent newspaper interview, "What do the good citizens want—law enforcement or dog enforcement?"

At first, the stray dogs were just a nuisance—making some noise and doing some property damage. However, when two children were reportedly attacked, several residents requested that the subdivision homeowners' association meet and discuss the problem.

Sam opened the meeting by reviewing what he and several other residents had experienced when they attempted to get local government help. Sam always involved himself in civic affairs, and this meeting was no exception. Throughout the meeting, he asked questions, made suggestions, and helped to settle disputes. For all his active behavior, Sam conducted himself in a very positive, thoughtful manner.

Carolyn, on the other hand, seemed constantly to inject either nonsense comments or personal opinions. For example, when Cliff, the father of one of the children attacked by the dogs, suggested that one step toward a solution would be for all the residents to keep their own dogs within fenced yards or inside, Carolyn burst out, saying, "That's not fair. Why should I keep my dogs tied up? I didn't move out here for that. Why don't you keep your kids tied up?"

Clark, who normally kept to himself, said that he would begin using poison bait if the problem weren't solved in one or two weeks. Unfortunately, that was Clark's only comment, since, before he could finish, Carolyn leaned across the table to call him an immoral killer of helpless animals.

Sam attempted to keep tempers cool by stating that he would gladly fence in his dogs or join in some kind of collection or trapping method so long as everyone agreed, but the group should try to be less emotional and focus on solving the problem rather than spend its time destroying neighborhood friendship.

(a) Which group members seemed to make a positive impression?

(b) Which group members participated the most?

(c) On the basis of good impression and participation, which group member is most likely to emerge as leader?

(a) Sam and Cliff; (b) Sam and Carolyn; (c) Sam

6. <u>Seating arrangement can also affect leadership emergence. If a group member is seated in a position that reduces face-to-face interaction with others, then participation becomes reduced and so does the possibility for emergent leadership.</u> Studies indicate that the group member who sits at the head of a rectangular table tends to interact more often than the other members. Placing oneself on the group's periphery (off to one side) may communicate to the group that you do not desire interaction. In some cases, a group member has little or no control over seating arrangement. He or she must then exert more effort to insure interaction. Whatever the physical arrangement of the meeting place, an individual who wishes to exercise leadership influence must place himself or herself in a position where the greatest amount of interaction occurs. The following example illustrates this point.

Case

Lester Burke saw Smitty walking down the hall and called to him, "Hey, Smitty! Can you come into my office for a minute?"

Smitty walked into Lester's office and sat down. "What do you need, Mr. Burke?"

"Smitty, I've just finished your report on the Consolidated Foods account, and I must say that it contains several very significant ideas. However, I can't understand why you didn't bring these points up at the staff meeting. If we could have had these ideas last week—well, you know..."

"Well, Mr. Burke," Smitty replied, "you didn't seem to show much interest in me at the last meeting. The entire staff seemed to hang on Reynold's every word, and I thought if you needed my opinion, you'd call on me."

"Come to think of it," Burke said, "I don't remember where you were sitting. Let's see, Reynolds was just to my left about where the arc of the table begins, Gordon was on the far end, Kirby and Conte were bunched up on my right. . ."

"You must remember," replied Smitty. "I sat over on the long sofa beneath the old man's picture. I always sit there because it's so comfortable, and you always say to make ourselves comfortable."

(a) In terms of position or seating, what was Smitty's problem?

(b) What are Smitty's chances of exerting leadership during the staff meetings if he continues to place his comfort above group interaction?

- - - - - - - - - - - - - - - - - - -

(a) Smitty placed himself in a position where no one noticed his presence.
(b) Not good. If he continues to sit on the sofa and keeps quiet, he simply will never have the chance to exert leadership.

LEADERSHIP STYLES

7. Besides examining leadership from the standpoint of its origin—appointed, assumed, or emergent—group leadership can also be studied in terms of leadership styles or how the leader interacts or behaves toward other group members. While researchers disagree on the number of basic leadership styles, our discussion of leadership in task-oriented, problem-solving groups will explore four styles of leadership behavior: authoritarian, democratic, laissez-faire, and nondirective.

Authoritarian leadership is most often associated with a high degree of control, structure, and direction. An authoritarian leader usually establishes and sets group goals and objectives, assigns member duties and tasks, monitors all phases of group activity, and makes or confirms the final decision. Traditionally, authoritarian leadership is cited as bad, or negative, leadership. Authoritarian leaders are described as lacking in trust for their fellows and as exploiting their own power and influence.

To some extent the criticism leveled at authoritarian leadership is valid. It fails to promote member participation in decision making, interaction, open discussion, member freedom, and creativity. Additionally, authoritarian leaders often exploit the group membership and abuse their own power and influence. However, authoritarian leadership sometimes best serves the interests of the group. For example, a group may find itself working against a time deadline, and the problem of time requires increased structure and direction, which can be provided through an authoritarian leadership style. The authoritarian style might also be desirable in cases of conflict between group members; the resolution of the conflict may rest upon an authoritarian decision when compromise or consensus cannot be achieved.

Laissez-faire leadership is the polar opposite of authoritarian leadership. Laissez-faire leaders make little attempt to exert control, structure, or direction over the activities of the group or its task. Unlike the authoritarian who doesn't seem to trust the group members, the laissez-faire leader does not seem to care one way or the other for the group members and the group task. Consequently, laissez-faire leaders may respond with indifference to group requests for feedback, support, and direction. If any advantage can be found in laissez-faire leadership, it might be the degree of freedom from close supervision experienced by the group members. Given the right group composition, laissez-faire leadership can produce a very creative group climate along with high levels of member satisfaction. However, a group that requires structure and direction or one that works under stress or pressure would experience great difficulty under a laissez-faire style of leadership.

A leader relying on the democratic leadership style seeks cooperation and participation from the group members and seeks to guide, not direct, the group's activities. Democratic leaders provide direction and structure as the situation requires, but they also encourage the group to develop or suggest procedures and operational methods. Democratic leaders are open to conflicting ideas and opinions and strive to maintain free-flowing communication. Leaders using the democratic style realize that the group members will be more committed to supporting and following decisions which they have shared in making, rather than decisions imposed by a leader. A democratic leader also conveys a positive attitude toward people. This attitude indicates to group members that they have worth, value, and ability, and that, given the chance, they can be highly productive and successful.

Democratic leaders do lead. Do not mistake the democratic leadership style as a reformed laissez-faire leadership. Democratic leaders are active and involved in the group process; they exert their influence, and the group members seek their direction. Democratic leaders share and spread their influence in an attempt to increase member participation, involvement, and sharing so as to produce a group consensus.

A variety of labels, such as nondirective, group-centered, and permissive, are used to describe a style of leadership where the leader does not direct, guide, or control. In nondirective leadership, the leader serves as a coordinator, a facilitator, and a sounding board. He or she attempts to maintain open communication channels among the group members by asking questions, redirecting questions, and summarizing and reviewing the progress of the group. If the group expresses a need for direction and structure, the nondirective leader will ask questions of the various group members, listen to their responses, and restate and reflect upon those responses, until the group charts its own direction and establishes its own controls. At no time would the nondirective leader impose his or her ideas or beliefs upon the group.

Nondirective leadership can be very frustrating and at times difficult for group members. However, the goal of nondirective leadership is to develop a climate where all group members exercise leadership and influence while, at the same time, the group makes all decisions regarding procedures, objectives, division of labor, problem solving, and so on. Do not confuse nondirective leadership with laissez-faire leadership. The nondirective leader is both very active and very concerned with the group and its progress. A nondirective style is probably the most difficult for a leader. Nondirective leaders must maintain the belief and attitude that the group can direct its own course and achieve success. They must hold back their own feelings and ideas and not fall prey to the temptation to assert control.

The business of leading discussions has probably occupied the attention of group members and researchers more than any other aspect of the discussion process. The leadership role most strongly affects the overall quality of the group discussion and its final product. How an individual acts in the leadership role often depends on the situation. Under different conditions, different types of leadership are most effective. A successful discussion-group leader will understand and recognize these differing situations and change leadership style as the situation dictates. Listed below are a number of factors that affect the group situation and thus the leadership style employed.

Leader personality factors: Since the person cannot be completely removed from the role, the leader's beliefs and values, attitudes toward people, and view of work accomplishment affect the style of leadership employed. A person who distrusts others may select an authoritarian style; a person who desires cooperation may select a democratic style; a person who wants the group to be self-directed (member-directed) may select a nondirective leadership style; a person who cares little for the group and accomplishing the task may become a laissez-faire leader.

Environmental factors: The environment or context within which the group operates affects leadership style. Time demands placed upon the group and the presence or absence of pressure or stress may call for alternative leadership styles. The leader of a newspaper editorial board may employ a more authoritarian style in getting the group to decide upon the content of the next day's edition than in planning feature stories for the next month.

Group-composition factors: The personality factors of the group members, their perception of appropriate leadership behavior, and their needs in terms of strong, moderate, mild, or nondirective supervision affect the choice of leadership style. College professors, due to their belief in academic freedom, often reject authoritarian leadership style and may force their department heads and administrators into democratic leadership styles.

Nature-of-task factors: The complexity or simplicity of the task and the limits of latitude or restriction placed upon suitable solutions affect leadership style. For example, a department store chain directs its marketing group to devise new ways of displaying merchandise to increase sales while maintaining optimum security against theft. The leader of such a group will need, in order to meet security requirements, to shift from a nondirective leadership intended to increase group creativity, to a more directive style.

What type of leadership style is best? No style is ideal for all situations. An effective leader must be able to recognize the best style of leadership for a situation. A leader must be flexible, adaptable, and able to adjust to the needs of the group, the context, and the task. For example, one condition affecting any group is the amount of time allocated for problem solution. An effective group leader will always consider the amount of time avialable in deciding upon the best type of leadership to employ. In general, the more time available for the group to transact its business, the less leadership control the group-discussion process requires, as the following case will illustrate.

Case
An American naval captain managing a European communications unit learned from the Pentagon several months in advance of a multimillion-dollar computer installation planned for his command. At the weekly staff meeting he announced the project, along with the details that were available, to the officers who managed specific departments within the command. The captain explained some of the problems that might be anticipated in the coming months and suggested that the officers begin working on ways to overcome them. He also asked them to bring up any new problems and to report developments on the computerization project at each weekly meeting. Their overall goal was to insure that the new facilities be installed and begin operating with no disruption to vital European defense communications.

As the target date for the project's completion approached, the captain began to give more specific directions about which problems were to be given priority. The attention of the most talented subordinate officers was directed to these problems. Meetings were held more than once a week, and frequently the weekends would find the captain and other group members busily working on the installation. The night of the scheduled switch to the automated system, all members of the group were in attendance. The captain's directions now became commands. The situation which had existed months earlier, when control over the group's progress could be left in the hands of each member, was behind them. At the switch-over, no time remained for discussion or speculation about how this or that problem might be handled. The captain controlled all the options, although the entire group actively participated in the actual switch.

(a)   How did the captain's leadership behavior change in the above case?

(b)   With regard to adaptable and flexible leadership, how does the captain fit our definition of appropriate leadership styles?

- - - - - - - - - - - - - - - - - -

(a)   As the time for problem solution grew short, the captain began to take more control over the process. His changes in leadership style were necessary due to the change in the situation facing the group.

(b)   The captain exerted different leadership styles according to the changing needs of the group. He did not maintain a single, uniform style of leadership.

8.   As the case in frame 7 shows, the amount of solution time available and the amount of control exercised by the leader are usually related. When the solution time is shortest, an authoritarian style is most effective, because control of the discussion process is focused on the leader. The authoritarian leader directs the discussion and takes an active part in determining which points should be considered and which discarded to speed the process.

An authoritarian leader is effective only to the extent that the group appreciates the conditions which lead to this exercise of control. A leader adopting the authoritarian style must be candid about those conditions to avoid discouraging the other group members. A leader who attempts authoritarian leadership when it is unwarranted may be ineffective and may even be rejected by the other group members. Thus, authoritarian leadership requires a form of consent by the group.

A style similar to authoritarian leadership, but not having its power based on the consent of the group, is known as bureaucratic leadership. A bureaucratic leader exercises power and influence due to the job or office he or she

holds. A production-line supervisor directs and controls the work of subordinates because a job description permits him or her to do so. While bureaucratic leaders may exercise great power and authority, their power and authority are based upon formal regulations or guidelines stipulated by the bureaucratic organization, which can replace the leader if bureaucratic authority is
abused.

In the case in frame 7, the captain asked other group members for suggestions and gave them considerable latitude in working on the problem when adequate time was available. That is, he exercised democratic leadership, the
type best suited to that occasion; he allowed each member of the group to contribute fully to both the group's operation and the overall task solution. If he
had wished, he could have led the group by using the bureaucratic style. His
position as a naval captain would fully permit his complete exercise of authority.
From the beginning of the project to its completion, he could have told his officers what guidelines and regulations had come down from Washington and
made assignments directed at solving each of the problems which came to his
attention without soliciting any input from them.

Clearly a senior naval officer has the authority to conduct the business of
his staff meetings in any way he desires. This commanding officer chose a
democratic leadership style when adequate time was available.

(a) By adopting a democratic style of leadership during the early stages of
the project, what did the captain allow his subordinate officers?

(b) What advantage would the captain gain from employing democratic leadership during the early stages of the project?

(c) At what point in the project did the captain exercise the most control over
the activities of the group?

(d) Place yourself in the role of one of the captains's subordinate officers.
Can you justify his use of direct control during the final states of the project?

- - - - - - - - - - - - - - - - - -

(a) He allowed them a chance to control their activities by sharing in the problem-solving process.

(b) He would receive more member participation and involvement and a wider
range of ideas and possible solutions to potential problems. His actions
might also improve morale, making members more satisfied with the process.

(c) At the switch-over point, the critical period of time when the new communications system was activated

(d) The captain's use of direct control can be justified in two ways: (1) His
bureaucratic authority would allow him such control, and (2) his behavior
was appropriate to the situation.

9. In the case of the naval captain, we saw a leader who altered and changed
his style of leadership as the group task requirements changed. When the captain desired full and widespread group participation, which included sharing
both ideas and decision making, he used a democratic style. When the group
approached the critical period leading to the switch-over, the captain assumed
an authoritarian leadership style. Clearly and without question, the captain
was the leader. Not all groups operate within a military command structure,
however; often group leaders emerge from within the membership. The style
of leadership is also affected by this situation. The following case illustrates
this point.

Case
Several years ago, a number of unmarked graves were discovered at a state
penal institution in the Southwest. The discovery was made shortly after a
new state administration had installed new directors in the state police and the
prison board. One television network affiliate in the area, Channel 4, was in-
strumental in breaking the story, and the news was widely reported.

After the national news media had finished its coverage, the Channel 4
news director decided to produce a documentary covering the circumstances
surrounding the discovery, the events that were prompted by the administrative
shake-ups, and the consequences for the people of the state. He called together several members of the news department and announced that he had arranged a thirty-minute time slot for a documentary based on the prison story,
to be broadcast in two weeks. In all, seven members of the news department
were assigned to the project; however, the seven were not to allow the project
to interfere with their daily assignments or to jepordize the quality of Channel
4's regular news programming. Even though the documentary required a
script, film and videotape editing, additional interviewing, and several trips
to the remote penal institution, two weeks was ample time to produce the show.

The news staff worked together at times, but much of their work was procedural and not really the product of a group discussion process. Their jobs
ranged from photographer to announcer, and they became members of the documentary group only for the purpose of producing this program. After reviewing the project with the documentary staff, the news director made one final
comment, "I'll be attending a News Directors' Association meeting this week,
and I'll be on special assignment the following week, so I expect you to get this
project done and not bother me until it's finished."

After the news director left the room, the documentary group sat quietly
for a few minutes; then the assignment editor said, "Well, how'd y'all want to
do this?"

What leadership style most describes the behavior of the news director—authoritarian, laissez-faire, democratic, or nondirective. Explain.

- - - - - - - - - - - - - - - - - -

laissez-faire. The news director does give orders somewhat in the manner of authoritarian style, but he makes it quite clear that the group is on its own; he's not going to be around, and he does not want the group members to bother him.

10. We might question the news director's behavior. If the documentary is such a good idea, why is he abandoning the leadership role? The group members are all highly skilled professionals in their individual specialties. However, if the director wants a creative approach to the prison story, he might need to oversee their day-to-day activity.

Besides a laissez-faire style of leadership, what other leadership types could the news director have used while still maintaining a climate for creative group involvement?

- - - - - - - - - - - - - - - - - -

Democratic leadership might work to some degree, but a nondirective approach seems to be the best alternative.

11. After the assignment editor asked, "How'd y'all want to do this?" a long, open discussion began. Topics ranged from possible scheduling conflicts to the best time for the group to meet again. The group spent more than an hour ironing out procedural and scheduling problems but still had not discussed the central problem—what would be the content or substance of the prison story? The assignment editor offered to recap the group's progress, and several other members agreed that a recap would be a good idea. The assignment editor reviewed what the group had covered during their discussion and then offered an observation. "Y'know, we're set on what to do, on how to do it, and where to go to do it, but we've not agreed on what it is we're doing." He then suggested that each staff member state what he or she felt to be the key elements for inclusion in the prison documentary; the members agreed to do so. This process took time, and there were many starts and stops, but every time the group became bogged down, the assignment editor reviewed and restated comments and redirected questions to keep the group progressing toward its goal.

By the end of the week, the documentary group was busily engaged in videotaping the interviews, film footage, and commentary segments of the production. On Monday of the following week, the group met to review all the materials which comprised the documentary. Again, each member offered his or her views on the final format and suggested last minute revisions and changes. When the group saw the final, edited videotape, they shared a sense of pride and accomplishment.

(a)   What signs of leadership are apparent in the news documentary group?

(b)   What type or style of leadership do you observe in the news documentary case?

(c)   Was the style of leadership you observed in the news documentary appropriate or inappropriate?

- - - - - - - - - - - - - - - - - - -

(a)   Other than the initial direction provided by the news director, the only other signs of leadership were those comments and suggestions provided by the assignment editor—since those comments influenced and helped the group chart its own course.
(b)   Laissez-faire for the news director and nondirective for the assignment editor.
(c)   While the laissez-faire style was inappropriate, the nondirective style was appropriate for this group of skilled and creative people who, under the right style of leadership, were capable of self-direction.

LEADERSHIP FUNCTIONS

12. Thus far, we have examined leadership in terms of leadership emergence and leadership styles. However, leadership can also be viewed as specific functions performed by one or more group members. Leadership functions are those procedural and coordinating activities that aid or shape the organization and structure of the group discussion. Functional leadership duties support the group and its task and should not be used to control or force the group's behavior.
    ✱ Functional leadership need not reside in one person. Functional leadership duties may be performed by any and all group members; as group priorities and needs change, so do the needs for functional leadership. The leadership functions may change hands several times during a single meeting, as various group members perform functions that place them in temporary leadership positions. A group member may satisfy an important group need regarding procedural requirements, for example, by initiating the discussion, attempting to maintain the agenda items to be discussed, and clarifying comments made by other members. Many groups operate on the principle of sharing such functions; other groups may delegate certain functions to an elected

chairman, to allow the group more time to concentrate on other concerns. In very formal, structured groups, such as many found in business, industry, and government committees, leadership duties are incorporated into the responsibilities of the committee chairman. Leadership functions can be divided into three broad categories: organizing, conducting, and concluding discussion activities.

Organizing duties involve prediscussion preparation and responsibilities that will later aid the group during its discussion process. A chairman appointed to a formal committee will need to develop a thorough understanding of the problem area and the committee's responsibility to the parent organization.

Suppose you were appointed to serve as chairman of the youth employment opportunities committee of a businesspersons' group. In such a position, you would need to know about youth employment and the authority of the committee—whether your committee is to study the subject, to make recommendations, or to implement the committee's decision or solution. Organizing duties are further illustrated in the following case.

Case
As the result of several serious work-realted accidents, the owners of Mid-States Building Supply Warehouse decided to enlist the aid of their warehouse workers in designing a safety program. Each of the six full-time warehouse employees was notified by a formal letter included in the weekly pay envelope. Along with a general explanation of the problem, the letter stated that the workers were free to discuss the problem in any manner they wished and that no management or supervisory personnel would interfere or try to oversee the employees' discussion. In addition, the warehouse would close one hour early on Saturday to allow the employees to meet.

At the initial meeting, the warehouse employees encountered several problems. Fred, one of the younger workers, wanted to know if group members would be given time off from work each week so they could develop the safety program. He said that he wasn't giving any of his free time to the boss. Ellen, the shipping clerk, reminded Fred that a good safety program would benefit them as well as management. Another worker, Curt, reread his copy of the letter and agreed with Fred; it did appear that the employees might have to meet on their own time in the future. Jose wanted to know if their union contract included safety rules and whether they should report their ideas to the union local before giving them to management. For a while, the group seemed to stall, unable to answer these questions. Finally, Sidney, another worker, said that he had to take the time sheets to the main office on Monday and, while there, he'd ask if they would be given additional work time to devote to the project; while he was downtown, he'd also stop at the union hall to find out what the contract said in regard to safety. The group members agreed that they would wait until after Monday before proceeding.

Which of the workers' comments, in the case above, most nearly indicates that one or more group members have assumend a functional leadership role?

- -

Sidney's comments about checking with management and the union

13. Sidney will be performing a valuable function, since what he learns will affect the group's future direction. Information such as the type sought by Sidney could also be useful in preparing an initial agenda of questions for group discussion and in providing a sharper orientation for the group members concerning their responsibility under the union contract.

Other organizing functions might include finding a meeting place and informing the membership of the time and location for the meeting. While concern over finding the best meeting place should never become more important than group problem solving, the work and comfort of the group can be enhanced by selecting a meeting place that conforms to the kind of work conducted by the group and the individual needs of group members. As we noted in Chapter 1, a meeting place should:

1. Provide adequate seating.

2. Be a comfortable environment for discussion in terms of lighting, temperature, space, noise, and visual stimuli.

3. Have room to accommodate any needed materials—audiovisual or writing materials or physical data such as reports to be reviewed, components to be examined, or parts to assemble.

Formal organizations often provide conference rooms for committee work, and only a reservation is necessary. For groups not belonging to formal organizations, the group chairman or some other group member will need to secure a meeting place. Such a meeting place should provide common access for for all group members, appropriate surroundings, and availability for future meetings.

What organizing duties might a functional leader perform for a group?

- - - - - - - - - - - - - - - - - -

Organizing duties involve prediscussion preparation and activities that will aid the group discussion process, such as prior understanding of the problem area, providing information which helps to orient the group gathering information related to the scope and responsibility of a formal group's task, preparation of a general agenda to use as a guide for discussion, locating a meeting place, and informing the group of the time and location for the meeting.

14. Conducting duties are leadership functions performed during the actual group discussion. Depending upon the nature of the group, a formal group chairman might assume responsibility for conducting duties, group members may share these duties, or individual members may perform certain conducting duties on an irregular or as-needed basis. Below is a list of several typical conducting functions.

> Initiating discussion: Providing a starting point; focusing attention on the problem at hand.

> Orientation: Introducing the topic and defining the purpose of discussion; reviewing previous meetings; focusing attention upon task issues.

> Monitoring agenda: Keeping track of the group's progress and digressions; keeping track of time if group sets limits or goals. For example, a leader might say, "Let's discuss this issue for an hour" or "...until we reach some agreement."

> Enhancing communication flow: Encouraging every member and providing each with an opportunity to participate.

> Establishing positive feelings: Reinforcing positive behavior; giving positive feedback where appropriate; accepting expressions of feelings from others; yeilding to divergent points of view or opinions without prejudice.

> Summarizing and providing transitions: Providing internal summaries or reviewing material covered, since group discussion can and does ramble, especially if the discussion drags on for a long time without the group's reaching decisions.

Remember, a group member who provides functional leadership by performing conducting duties satisfies an important need of the group by facilitating certain procedural requirements. Such duties may be highly structured and routine, as in the case of a formal committee chairperson, or they may be simple verbal comments. In either case, functional leadership acts are important due to their influence on the group discussion process. The interaction between group members in the following example should help to clarify this point.

Case
Just before the meeting was to start, Richard was entertaining Roger and Walt with his well-known John Travolta imitation. Although he could see that both Roger and Walt were enjoying the show, Paul asked Richard to be quiet so the meeting could begin.

(a) How would you classify Paul's comment to Richard?

(b) What circumstances would need to be present in order for the other participants (Richard, Roger, and Walt) to approve of Paul's actions?

- - - - - - - - - - - - - - - - - -

(a)   Paul is attempting to exert functional leadership by conducting duty.
(b)   Paul would have to satisfy a felt need of the group, a need for procedural leadership.

15. Look at the conducting procedures in the context of a more formal group— a jury.

Juror 1:   Shouldn't we get started?
Juror 2:   Yeah, it's late.
Foreman: Well, ah, I guess you're right, Can I have your attention? Please sit down.
Juror 3:   Should we sit by number, or will any seat do?
Foreman: Well, ah, ah, right, by numbers. One here, two next, three next, and so on. Does anyone have anything to say? I think you all know what we're supposed to do?
Juror 4:   Aren't we supposed to take a preliminary vote first?
Juror 2:   Yeah, let's vote and see where everyone stands.
Foreman: OK, let's take a vote. Juror 1, how do you vote?*

In this example, did the foreman aid or inhibit the proceedings of the group? Explain.

- - - - - - - - - - - - - - - - - -

The foreman's conducting methods were poor and probably delayed the group's progress. A jury is a formal type of decision-making group with rather well-established procedures. The jurors appeared to know better than the foreman what was required to begin the decision-making task. The foreman could improve his performance by coming to the jury room with a better understanding of his conducting duties.

16. Now look at the conducting procedures in this evaluating committee:

Chairperson: Ms. Reed will be five minutes late, but I feel that we can go ahead and get started. From the memo sent to you last week, I trust that you all know what our task is. Personally, I think it's a good program, and I can see no major changes forthcoming other than minor refinements. Also I feel that if we are

---

*This sequence of comments was suggested by a situation in the television play Twelve Angry Men by Reginald Rose. Copyright © 1956 by Reginald Rose.

	systematic about this, we can all get home early tonight. Now does anyone have anything additional to offer?

Member X: I agree with you that, in general, the program is a good one, but I see two areas of the internal report which indicate to me a weakness regarding staffing and staff development.

Chairperson: I'll note your remarks; Now, Member Y, do you have anything to offer?

Member Y: I'd like to follow up on what was just said concerning staff...

Chairperson: Well, now, let's not beat a dead horse. Let's proceed around the table and see if we have any new observations to make.

Member Z: I did, but I'll pass!

Did the chairperson aid or inhibit the proceedings of the group? Explain.

- - - - - - - - - - - - - - - - - -

The chairperson inhibited this group's proceedings. This chairperson is the opposite of the jury foreperson. While the jury foreperson was disorganized and easy-going, the chairperson of this group performed in a highly sturctured manner. He seemed in a great rush to finish the activities of the group, and his conducting procedures retarded the free flow of ideas and comments. Members of the group received terse responses from the chairperson with little indication that he wanted to hear what they had to say.

17. Now look at the conducting procedures in this community betterment group:

Chairperson: This group is meeting for the first time since four of us mutually discovered a common interest in developing a community betterment organization. I hope this group will form the basis of a larger organization to carry on the work of building a better community. I see that our original group of four has grown to seven. For the benefit of our new members, I'll briefly review the series of informal discussions which lead to the formation of this group...

Glen: Thanks for the review. I'd like to add a few things concerning other betterment groups in the state.

Chairperson: Sure, go right ahead.

Glen: The first community betterment group was formed at...

Marge: Thanks, Glenn, for that background information. I drove to the capital this week and obtained some literature from the state

	community betterment association which might be helpful in forming our group.
Chairperson:	It was good of you to do that Marge. That material might answer a few questions or provide some ideas on how to get started.
Marge:	I've also made copies of this information which I'll pass around.
Chuck:	Why don't we take five minutes to look through the material Marge brought? It might stimulate some questions.
Chairperson:	Seems like a good suggestion, but let's ask the rest of the group members—should we take five minutes and read the materials? Bob, you've been a bit silent. Is this idea all right with you?
Bob:	Thanks for asking. I didn't want to barge in, this being the first time I've met with the whole group, but I feel that our time might be better spend if Marge would just summarize the material and let us read it when we get home.
Helen:	Why not just read it here and get it over with?
Chairperson:	Before we get into an argument, let's ask Marge for her opinion. After all, she provided the information.

(a) Did the chairperson aid or inhibit the proceedings of the group? Explain.

(b) What other members of this group performed functional leadership duties? Explain.

- - - - - - - - - - - - - - - - - -

(a) The chairperson aided the proceedings. In this example, we see a chairperson who performs certain conducting functions without completely dominating the group. The chairperson introduced the purpose of the meeting and gave a brief orientation. In addition, we see the chairperson encouraging a member (Glen) to proceed, giving praise (to Marge), and asking for the group's opinion rather than telling the group what to do. Finally, the chairperson forestalls a possible argument between Helen and Bob.

(b) Glen provided additional orientation by reviewing information concerning other community betterment groups. Marge obtained additional information that could be used to help organize the group's activities. Marge also made copies of her information. Chuck made a suggestion concerning how the group should structure its time. Bob also made a suggestion concerning how the group should proceed.

18. As each member performs functions that satisy group needs, he or she gains respect from other participants, according to the quality and quantity of the contributions. In addition, the more respect an individual builds for himself or herself, the more that person's deviance from the group norm is tolerated. In other words, the participant who has provided leadership in facilitating the discussion will be able to defy the group's standards and beliefs more effectively and more often than the member who has contributed little or nothing to the group. The successful group member should remember, however, that in deviating from the group norms, he or she will lose the respect of other members. Thus even a person who is well liked and has contributed much to the group effort may find other participants turning a "cold shoulder" toward him or her if he or she persists in advocating an unpopular notion.

What we find, then, is a circular relationship between leadership, leadership functions, and the group's task accomplishment. Since leadership is often viewed as being functions that support the group and help achieve its goal, and groups view individuals who perform those functions as leaders, people desiring leadership roles would be wise to perform functions that will facilitate the group discussion process.

Concluding duties involve providing a sense of closure or finality to the various portions of the group proceedings. Often overlooked are internal summaries which are useful as the group shifts from one area to another or after a decision has been accepted, before moving on to new topics or proposals. Final summaries at the end of a discussion session are also useful and fall into the category of concluding duties. Such final summaries serve as a recap or review of the proceedings which helps to refresh the group's memory of just what has taken place and been decided. In formal committee proceedings, the chairperson is responsible for seeing that a summary is made and that a written copy of the summary is sent to each group member. In less formal group discussions, one or more group members can provide functional leadership by offering to summarize what the group has accomplished.

The next two examples will help to illustrate concluding procedures.

(a) Richard took his responsibility as group chairman very seriously—so seriously that he summarized after each member's contribution. Do you feel that Richard's summarizing after every contribution falls into the category of concluding duties?

(b) Harold's group had been meeting for over three hours, and the time seemed well spent. Several issues confronting the group had been discussed and dealt with. However, at this point, the group members seemed to be winding down, and their enthusiasm appeared to be waning, even though they had accomplished many things. The members' faces almost seem to say, "Let's get this over for tonight." If you were Harold, how might you exert functional leadership?

- - - - - - - - - - - - - - - - - -

(a) No. By being overzealous, Richard was actually hindering the group's
     work.
(b) Harold could provide functional leadership by offering to review what the
     group had accomplished and asking the other members to set a time and
     place for the next meeting. If Harold acted in this manner, he would pro-
     vide closure in the formal sense and satisfy a felt need (expressed through
     facial expressions) to reaffirm decisions reached and end the meeting.

SUMMARY

Leadership is one of the most important roles in group problem-solving discussion. Often the success or failure of the group discussion process hinges
on the nature of the leadership present within the group. In general, leadership may be defined as any act or behavior that affects the group's climate,
process, problem solving, and decision making. Efforts to describe group
leadership focus upon various characteristics and dimensions of leadership.

While leaders are often appointed or assume authority, in many cases
leaders emerge from within the group itself. Characteristics such as physical
size, age, attractiveness, and intelligence can propel a group member into a
leadership role. In addition, a group member who is willing to work, prepare,
contribute ideas, make a good impression, participate actively, and be concerned with seating arrangement can also emerge as the group leader.

A leader's behavior and attitude toward the group and the group process
is described in terms of leadership style. An authoritarian style of leadership
is most associated with a high degree of leader control, direction, and supervision; so is the closely related bureaucratic style. Laissez-faire leaders exert little control and direction over the activities of the group. Group members serving under laissez-faire leaders experience a high degree of freedom.
A leader exercising democratic leadership style seeks cooperation and participation from the group members. Democratic leaders provide direction and
structure as required but encourage the group to develop, or suggest procedures, operational methods, and free-flowing communication patterns. The
nondirective leader attempts to stimulate the group toward self-direction. A
nondirective leader does not impose his or her ideas or beliefs upon the group.

Successful group leadership also involves performing various procedural
and coordinating functions. These functional aspects of leadership involve
such things as organizing, conducting, and concluding the discussion. The ob-
ject of functional leadership is to facilitate the group process and not to command or control the group members.

While ideal leadership models are easy to describe, successful leadership
is often the product of the situation, the group personality, and the task. Thus,
individuals desiring leadership roles should be adaptable and flexible.

SELF-TEST

The following questions will help you assess how well you understand the material in Chapter 6. Answer the questions, and then look at the answers and review instructions that follow.

1. As chairperson of the budget committee, Stacy feels that she must carefully supervise and direct the members of her group. Stacy provides all group procedures and makes any decisions. What style of leadership is Stacy exhibiting?

2. After thirty years of service, Roger leads his final fire-cause investigation group. His last case presents little challenge: A vacant warehouse already scheduled for demolition has burned following a thunder storm. Roger remains in his car as the investigation group surveys the fire scene. From time to time, members of the group tap on the car window and ask Roger for advice. Roger responds by waving them off. What style of leadership is Roger exibiting?

3. List three involuntary factors contributing to leadership emergence.

    (a)

    (b)

    (c)

4. You have been appointed chairman of a marketing and advertising committee. The purpose of the committee is to develop a sales campaign for a new product. However, in order to beat the competition, the product must be on the market within six weeks. Your group is comprised of highly talented and creative people. You need the full cooperation of the group in order to launch the best possible sales campaign. Which leadership style would be best for you to use?

5. An individual wishes to improve his or her chances of emerging as group leader. What kinds of behaviors or other factors might help this person in that quest?

6. A group leader is observed asking questions, encouraging participation, and providing needed background information. What kind of leadership function is this leader performing?

7. When we speak of "organizing" leadership duties, we are referring to what?

Answers to Self-Test

Compare your answers to the questions on the Self-Test with the answers given below. If you had difficulty with any questions, you may want to review the frames indicated in parentheses following the answer. If you miss several questions, you should probably reread the entire chapter carefully.

1. authoritarian leadership (frames 7-11)

2. laissez-faire leadership (frames 7-11)

3. physical size, age, intelligence, or attractiveness (frames 1-6)

4. Democratic leadership would best serve your purpose. (frames 7-11)

5. Leadership emergence may be enhanced through willingness to work, preparation, contribution of ideas, making a good impression, active participation, and improving seating position in relation to group interaction patterns. (frames 1-6)

6. procedural and coordinating functions (frames 12-18)

7. Organizing leadership duties include: A leader's preparation for the discussion, providing needed background information, and finding a meeting place. (frames 12-18)

Final Test

We hope that, through this book, you have acquired some skills that will make your group problem-solving endeavors more successful. We firmly believe that the greater your understanding of communication and the group discussion process, the more effective you will be in a group setting.

The Final Self-Test that follows will help you see how well you have mastered the major concepts in the book. The test includes some general questions and four case studies; correct answers and review instructions follow the test.

Our aim has been to help you solve problems and make decisions more effectively, whatever your group situation. We hope that Communication for Problem Solving is a first step in that direction. Now it is up to you to apply your new skills and make them your own.

The following Self-Test will help you assess how well you understand the material in this book. Answer the questions, and then look at the correct answers and review instructions that follow.

1. What is brainstorming, and what are its potential strengths and weaknesses?

2. What are the strengths and weaknesses of a systematic versus a nonsystematic approach to problem solving?

3. What distinguishes a problem-solving discussion group from other groups and collections of individuals?

4. What are the advantages of group problem-solving discussion over individual problem solving?

5. How would you answer the criticism that a group takes more time to solve a problem than an individual would take?

6. Explain the difference between public and private group discussion.

7. What are the three major types of public discussion formats, and what are the basic characteristics of each?

8.   Briefly describe the organizing duties of a discussion leader.

9.   Briefly describe the conducting duties of a discussion leader.

10. Briefly describe the concluding duties of a discussion leader.

11. The systematic approach to problem solving has two phases.   Identify them.

12. Identify the steps within each of the two phases of the systematic approach
     to problem solving.

13. Why is it dangerous to be solution-oriented before a problem has been
     properly explored?

Case A: Alpha Sales

Alpha Sales supplies nonperishable goods to independent supermarkets and
grocers. The company has grown from a small, family-run business to a large,
regional wholesale firm. When the company began, the immediate family members and a few part-time employees conducted the entire business. Today, the
sales territory has increased from one urban area to a four-state region. At
present, over two hundred full-time and salaried employees work for Alpha
Sales. Several of the original part-time employees have risen over the years
to management positions; however, Wayne Davis, the founder of the company
still holds close control of the day-to-day operations.

     Lately, the growth of the company has leveled out, and in some sales dis-
tricts, orders have declined. In addition, Alpha has experienced a large turnover of field representatives. A former sales representative stated that his
orders were constantly incomplete or late. The same representative sent complaints directly to Davis, but this method failed to get results, since Davis
was often too busy to foward the information to the shipping department.

     Davis has recognized that his company is experiencing problems and has
tried to discover the reasons for the decline, but, to this date, he has failed to
do so. Davis prides himself on the fact that he runs every aspect of the company.

14. How have the problems at Alpha Sales surfaced?

15. What approach to problem solving has been used so far at Alpha Sales?

16. By attempting to solve all the company's problems by himself, Davis has failed to make use of what?

17. If Davis asked you for your advice on how to solve the problems confronting his company, what would you suggest?

Case B: Zoning Commission Subcommittee

The business and commercial subcommittee of the county zoning commission began its first meeting sharply at 7:00 p.m. Since most of the members were newly appointed, few, if any, of the members had previously met. This being the case, the members of the zoning commission possessed only limited knowledge of what roles and responsibilities service on the subcommittee could require. Robert Greer, the lone elected zoning commissioner on the subcommittee, assumed the leadership role. Greer called the meeting to order and read the names of the committee members.

"Gerald Constance." "Present."
"Margaret Jordan." "Here."
"Ted Graham." "Present."
"Jose Ganzales." "Here."
"Susan Carmichael." "Present."
"W. C. Jones." "Here."

After taking attendance, Greer handed Susan a note pad and requested that she serve as the recording secretary.

18. Based only on what we know about the zoning subcommittee, why would Robert Greer be allowed to assume the leadership role?

19. Susan's job as recording secretary might be described in a different manner. What term might we apply to Susan's job?

20. Of all the members of the subcommittee, why do you suppose Greer selected a woman to serve as recording secretary?

21. Suppose that Greer had included the profession or occupation of each committee member as he called his or her name.

"Gerald Constance, president of Constance and Associates, General Contractors."
"Margaret Jordan, executive director of Retail Merchants Association."
"Jose Gonzales, manager, City Center Hotel."
"Ted Graham, English teacher, West County High School."
"Susan Carmichael, M.D., County General Hospital."
"W. C. Jones, retired merchant and president of Senior Citizens' Social Action Club."

Would role expectations have differed?

Case C: Halfway House

As students began wandering into the Halfway House, Pete Norman could not resist remembering with pride the success of the past year. When he had begun his ministry at University Church, there had been little to attract the students to his church. By going to the dormitories, the Greek houses, the student union, and the streets, he had attracted a gathering of students ranging from those studying for the ministry to the long-haired, barefooted kids who aimlessly played guitars and sang in Logan Park. Somehow they had saved their meeting place, a white frame house near the campus, from the clutches of urban renewal. Progress was slow at first, but by the end of his first year, Pete had achieved some success in bringing together the "Jesus freaks" and the "straights" from the organized church.

Tonight the group was meeting to discuss the movie Jesus Christ Superstar, which was playing at a local movie house. Earlier the students had decided that they wanted to give people a chance to see the movie and then have an open house house to discuss the film. Letters to the editors of the local and campus newspapers had labeled the picture everything ranging from "sinful" to "magnificent." Tonight about fifteen Halfway House people were gathered to talk. Their task wa was to try to get their feelings about the movie out in the open so that they could could compose their own letter to the editor of the campus newspaper.

Pete had found that the best way to operate was for him to be a member of the group—he never encouraged the kids to call him "Dr. Norman." If they were gathered for discussion and a large number showed up, he would suggest that they break up into smaller groups so that everyone felt that he or she had a part to play in the activity. He never attempted to impose rules on the people, feeling that they could more effectively achieve their goals if they agreed to their own rules as they progressed. Pete had discovered that the students at first were ineffective as a group; only after they had begun to understand and respect each other did they begin to draw together as a group.

Tonight they sat sprawled on the floor in excited conversation. "Hold it," Ellen Lake said. "We can't all talk at once." She was one of the so-called street people, but she had the deep respect of the group. Her long hair and "way out" manner of dress had turned off many of the others at first. However, Ellen had a fine mind, and she knew how to express herself. She had gained respect from many of the kids who saw her as a leader, but not a dictator, she was able to keep people talking, while moving toward some goal.

During this session Pete watched Don Harding rather closely. Don did not have the respect of the group. He was new to college and to religion and was having a difficult time with life in general. The few times that he had attempted to become involved in a discussion, he had discovered that he did not know what what he was talking about; the group had "shot him down." Pete desperately wanted Don to feel that his ideas were acceptable to others. He hoped that eventually Don would begin to interact successfully with the others. For the moment, however, Don sat and listened.

As the discussion progressed, a conflict developed. Jim Hawkins, a Black, raised a point: The movie was racist, because Judas was portrayed by a Black man. Greg Caldwell, one of the "straights" in the group, took immediate exception to the issue. "Oh, bull, do we have to get into this?" Greg's thinking had been liberalized by his time in college and as a member of this group. However, he was not ready to find racial insults behind everything. An argument developed between the two men. The "street people," who normally reinforced Jim, sided with Greg. They were so taken by the movie's music as a religious experience that they were not concerned with the race of any of the actors. The other two Blacks, who were more conservative than Jim, failed to give him more than token support. Jim, who could see that he had lost the issue, became hostile toward Greg who had thwarted his efforts to determine the course of the discussion.

Pete saw that this conflict could destroy the purpose of the meeting and have a devastating effect on the entire Halfway House concept. If racial disharmony were to develop, all he had worked for was in danger of being destroyed. To keep the group intact, he moved cautiously to find something about which the two combatants could agree. He began talking about the role of Judas. Had not the priests of the temple taken advantage of Judas's human qualities and his fear of what Jesus might be doing to the movement? he pointed out. The fact that Judas was Black could have been by design. "How long have we seen Whites take advantage of the honest intentions of Blacks?"

Pete was not certain if this point could legitimately be made about the movie; however, it did relieve a degree of conflict. Greg agreed that, in that context, he could see a basis for a racial discussion. "In fact," he added, "that could explain why both the role and songs of Judas were so powerful." He concluded, "There is no doubt that the Black is a powerful figure in America and that the Black has been forced to express much of that power in the form of music."

"Right on, baby," was Jim's reply.

While some hostility remained between Jim and Greg, the immediate crisis had been abated. The discussion moved from this to other points concerning the religious experiences to be gained from seeing the movie.

Pete did not know if the group would ever reach the point where they could put all of its thoughts into a letter. Only the ensuing discussion would determine if the group was sufficiently cohesive to actually reach the letter-writing stage. He did know that they would never be a complete group until they determined a way to make Don feel a part. But they were still together, and they were talking. Pete believed they were moving forward.

22. What style of leadership was Pete (Dr. Norman) using? Explain.

23. What leadership characteristics did Pete manifest? Explain.

24. What group building and maintenance role was Ellen playing when she exclaimed: "Hold it. We can't all talk at once." Explain.

25. What signs of tension were shown by the group? How were they handled?

Case D: The Library

For several years, students and faculty at a northeastern college complained that library materials were being mutilated. Sections of magazine and journal articles were snipped out, and pages from books were torn from the bindings; in some cases, whole chapters were missing. The students complained to their professors, and the professors complained to the library staff, but the problem continued. Everyone concerned with the problem suggested solutions, but no coordinated action followed. Each group involved—the students, the faculty, and the library staff—shifted the responsibility to someone else.

Finally, a group of speech communication majors, enrolled in a group-discussion and decision-making course, decided to put theory into practice. Recognizing that the problem of mutilated books, papers, and journals affected all members of the college community, these students organized a problem-solving group discussion.

As students they shared a common frustration of discovering mutilated source materials. However, they realized that the faculty and the library staff should also take part in the proceedings of the problem-solving discussion group. Two student representatives of the original group assumed the task of recruiting faculty and library staff members to meet with them.

26. In Case D, what was the problem?

27. What campus groups could provide participants for a problem-solving discussion?

28. Who recognized the general nature of the problem?

29. What was the first step before any problem-solving group could possibly be formed?

30. What decision by the students demonstrated their understanding of the general nature of the problem?

31. Before this group can discuss possible solutions to the library problem, several things need to be done. What might they include?

32. From the information provided, what type of discussion group is the student-faculty-library staff group?

33. If the participants of the group present their findings and solutions to a convocation of the entire college community, then we could describe this group as what type of discussion group?

ANSWERS TO FINAL TEST

Compare your answers to the questions on the Final Self-Test with the answers given below. If all your answers are correct, you have a good understanding of the of the material presented in this book. If you had difficulty with any questions, you may want to review the sections indicated in the parentheses following the answer. If you missed several questions, you should probably reread the entire book carefully.

1. Brainstorming is a technique for stimulating the generation of ideas and facilitating their expression. It is a creative tool which can be of great assistance in generating sheer quantity of ideas available for consideration in problem solving. From a quantity of ideas, greater quality is likely to surface; however, a group must be capable of separating the useless from the useful for the technique to be helpful. Brainstorming does not operate well under a deadline, and much silence along with a healthy measure of

completely useless ideas should be expected. Moreover, in many situations where criteria and potential solutions are so clearly established that brainstorming might be frustrating, since the results of this process could not be used. (Chapter 3, frames 7-9)

2. Systematic problem solving is best when time is at a premium, when the group is relatively large, and when a rational, carefully planned approach is needed (which is most of the time). However, rigid structure may stifle creative thinking, so problem-solving approaches should maintain flexibility. When strong feelings are expressed, a nonsystematic approach may work best to provide more freedom and flexibility. However, a lack of structure can often lead to chaos, so the group should realize why a systematic approach has been abandoned and make efforts to return to a systematic approach when the nonsystematic approach is no longer needed. (Chapter 3, frames 1, 20)

3. A problem-solving discussion group involves the elements of sharing, participating, and interacting. Unlike other groups it involves a decision-making process. (Chapter 1, frames 1-3)

4. An individual solves a problem solely on the basis of his or her own knowledge and experience, assumes the labor and responsibility required, and then carries out the decision. The individual may or may not make the right decision, but the entire burden rests upon his or her shoulders. Group problem solving uses the ideas and experiences of several people. In addition, a group can share labor and responsibility and make more efficient use of human resources. Also, ideas can be tested and improved in the group before the decision is enacted. (Chapter 1, frames 7-15)

5. The criticism is actually invalid. If a fast decision needs to be made, as in an emergency, then a group approach should not be used. However, the goal of the group problem-solving discussion is quality solutions, not speed; such a group may spend more time, but it is spent in pursuit of quality solutions. (Chapter 1, frames 7-15)

6. Private discussion groups meet in private to make decisions and solve problems. Public discussions meet in the presence of an audience for the purpose of informing, stimulating, or persuading the audience. (Chapter 1, frames 16-20)

7. In a panel discussion, a group of individuals—experts or laypeople—engage in a face-to-face discussion of a problem or an issue. Panels tend to be spontaneous and free-wheeling. An audience is present during a panel discussion.

   In a symposium discussion, a group of individuals each present a prepared speech on a segment of the discussion topic. The participants in a symposium discussion do not interact with the other members of the group. An audience is present durning a symposium.

   A forum discussion format involves a large group of people engaging in discussion as the result of some other activity, such as a town meeting, a lecture, or a panel discussion. (Chapter 1, frames 23-26)

8. Organizing duties involve prediscussion preparation and responsibilities such as developing knowledge of the problem, preparing an agenda, arranging for a meeting place, informing the group members of the time and location of the meeting, and orienting members. (Chapter 6, frames 12-13)

9. Conducting duties include calling the meeting to order, introducing the topic and purpose of the discussion, monitoring the agenda, stimulating responses, enhancing communication flow, establishing positive feelings, and summarizing and providing transitions. (Chapter 6, frames 14-17)

10. Concluding duties involve providing a sense of closure to the group proceedings. These duties might include giving a final summary or overview of the group's accomplishments for a given session. In some instances, the chairperson is responsible for providing a written summary of the meeting for each group member. (Chapter 6, frame 18)

11. problem-description phase and problem-solution phase (Chapter 3, frames 3-7)

12. The problem-description phase has two steps: definition and limitation of the problem, and analysis of the problem. The problem-solution phase has four steps: generation of possible solutions; appraisal of possible solutions; selection of the best solution; and implementation of the solution. (Chapter 3, frames 3-7)

13. Offering solutions to a problem before it is thoroughly defined, limited, and analyzed can be disasterous. Common understanding of the terms and limits of the problem plus a thorough analysis should yield insights that would be missed if solutions were discussed prematurely. Just as no one wants a "knife-happy" surgeon, we should be careful to consider fully a problem before exploring solutions. (Chapter 3, frames 3-5)

Case A: Alpha Sales
14. Business has leveled off, sales have declined, and employee turnover has been great.

15. an individual approach

16. Human resources. Alpha has over two hundred employees, several of whom have been with the company since its founding. Seemingly others could contribute to the problem-solving process.

17. Davis is trying to do too many things by himself. He needs to open channels of communication with his employees. A problem-solving discussion group presents one such means of opening communication. In addition, the participation of employees in a problem-solving group would ease Davis's load and perhaps give him additional time, which he seems to need.
(For questions 14-17 review Chapter 1, if necessary.)

Case B: Zoning Commission Subcommittee

18. Since Greer was the only elected official, a group such as the zoning sub-committee might naturally expect him to take charge.

19. role

20. Society, which is a super-group, often typecasts or stereotypes roles by sex. Until recent times, females were likely to serve as secretaries—it was an expected role.

21. Yes, they might. Roles might be allocated according to interests and abilities rather than sex.
(For questions 15-18, review Chapters 5 and 6, if necessary.)

Case C: Halfway House

22. Pete (Dr. Norman) was using a nondirective style of leadership. Serving as a coordinator and facilitator, he was able to maintain open communication channels among group members by asking and redirecting skillful questions. His efforts to defuse the conflict about Judas being Black and to become more of a member of the group are two prime indicators of the nondirective style of leadership. (Chapter 6, frames 7-11)

23. Pete manifested the characteristics of (1) a listener as he listened carefully on a verbal as well as nonverbal level. This characteristic was especially visible in Pete's observation of Don Harding. (2) When conflict emerged concerning the color of Judas, Pete used questioning effectively in examining reasons why the role of Judas may have been played by a Black man. (3) His initiating skills were apparent in efforts to improve the relations between and among the Halfway House people. (Chapter 5, frame 7)

24. Ellen was playing the role of a gatekeeper, keeping the communication channels open by encouraging or facilitating the participation of others. (Chapter 5, frames 17, 19, 21)

25. Primary tension may have been present in Don. He was new in the group and appeared to lack confidence in himself. This primary tension was not being handled, but more time spent in socializing activities might help Don feel more comfortable with the group.
Secondary tension is evident in Jim's unsupported bid for leadership influence. Hidden agendas might have been involved in Jim's predisposition to see racist overtones in the movie being discussed. To lessen the hostility between Jim and Greg, Pete attempted to find areas of agreement. While this seemed to help, more time would have to be spent discussing the sources of the hostility in an open and honest fachion. (Chapter 2, frames 2-4)

Case D: The Library

26. mutilated library materials

27. students, faculty, and library staff

28. some speech communication students

29. problem recognition

30. They sought faculty and library staff to meet with them, to broaden the membership base of the group.

31. They need a place to meet and some basic organization, including an agenda.

32. a private problem-solving discussion group

33. public
(For questions 23-31, review Chapters 1 and 4, if necessary.)

Index

NOTES